# The Politics of
# New Communities

# Wayt T. Watterson
# Roberta S. Watterson

The Praeger Special Studies program—utilizing the most modern and efficient book production techniques and a selective worldwide distribution network—makes available to the academic, government, and business communities significant, timely research in U.S. and international economic, social, and political development.

# The Politics of New Communities

## A Case Study of San Antonio Ranch

PRAEGER SPECIAL STUDIES IN U.S. ECONOMIC, SOCIAL, AND POLITICAL ISSUES

**Praeger Publishers**    New York    Washington    London

Library of Congress Cataloging in Publication Data

Watterson, Wayt T
   The politics of new communities.

   (Praeger special studies in U. S. economic, social
and political issues)
   Bibliography: p.
   Includes index.
   1.   Cities and towns—Planning—San Antonio.  2.  New
towns—Case studies.  I.  Watterson, Roberta S., joint
author.  II.  Title.
HT168.S195W38      309.2'62'09764351      75-15509
ISBN 0-275-08260-1

PRAEGER PUBLISHERS
111 Fourth Avenue, New York, N.Y. 10003, U.S.A.

Published in the United States of America in 1975
by Praeger Publishers, Inc.

Printed in the United States of America

In April 1973, San Antonio Ranch New Town (SAR) became the first federally assisted new community to be drawn into a court action that would determine ultimately whether it could be built as planned. This significant trial was the culmination of more than two years of bitter and divisive conflict over SAR, chiefly in San Antonio, but extending as well to Austin and Washington. The issues and actors were many and diverse, some well-defined and others covert, but almost all were polarized and irreconcilable. What evolved was a classic political confrontation over the "new" topic of a large new community, the impact and results of which may be felt for a long time in San Antonio and in the federal new community program.

Very little is "new" in the concept of new communities, of which some fifty to one hundred are currently in some phase of construction in the United States, mainly as private entrepreneurial efforts backed by real estate or corporate interests. What is new is the assistance and participation of the federal government in new community planning and development as part of national public policy. In the SAR case, many elements of that policy were questioned in terms of priorities, constituencies, available options, and ultimate impacts.

The foundation for such political confrontations was set by the Urban Growth and New Community Development Act of 1970 (Title VII of the Housing and Urban Development Act). Under the Act, private land developers could qualify for loan guarantees and grants for new community development, but not before intensive review of the proposed project by HUD staff and at least perfunctory approval by the local and regional governments which would eventually be responsible for such matters as zoning, utilities, and schools. Consequently, a complex system of public-private and intergovernmental relations was established, in which the initiative comes from the private sector and the financial strength and project control from the federal level, but the ultimate benefits and burdens falling on the local and regional governments and their constituents.

As yet the dynamics and impacts on local areas of this new and unique public-private partnership have not been adequately documented or studied. This case study of San Antonio Ranch attempts to add to the literature on this partnership on three different levels. At the first of these, it contains a documentary history of SAR from its inception as a developmental idea through its trial on environmental, social, and procedural grounds. Not only is such a history needed as an impartial record that cuts through the confusion of this unusual and significant case, but also, through the process of gathering together scraps of evidence, the underlying causes and reasons for the sequence of events can be better understood. The record itself is essentially a journalistic endeavor, with all the attendant risks of error and fallibility.

On a second level, the study relates the events and their causes to a framework of theory in politics and decision making for each layer of government involved—local, regional, state, and federal. In each case the processes and outputs are identified and analyzed in terms of the SAR experience. On the local level, the analysis concentrates on the role of SAR in the transition from consensus to conflict in politics. The analysis also focuses on the pervasive federal impact on the form and functional priorities of local areas and the dynamics of citizen opposition to new communities—a new and expanding phenomenon since the SAR experience.

The third tier of this study is an analysis of the SAR case in terms of new community development in general, and Title VII new communities in particular. Ultimately the pivotal issue with respect to SAR was that of the public interest—who defines it, who represents it, and who is affected by it? This issue has pervaded debate on almost all new communities to date, both in regard to governmental relations and in the evolution of systems of governance. What has been clouded in the Title VII process is the reality of the new communities as major federal project actions, with unrealized policy potential as well as with significant and lasting impacts. As such they are far too important to be left to traditional real estate development mechanisms locally, or to haphazard citizen opposition. Intergovernmental controls and broad participation are needed to define, represent, and uphold the public interest. Processes once established can then benefit conventional new community development as well. A model process toward these ends is proposed as a conclusion to this study.

The study itself ranges quite broadly. The actors involved include the large developer team, various agencies and individuals at the local, regional, state, and federal governmental levels, interested private groups and individuals, and those affected by the SAR project but not directly involved in it. The issues concern land development, governmental powers and controls, federal policies and impacts, political decision making on various levels, the physical environment as a public resource, and new communities as hybrids of large subdivisions and urban growth policy.

The study therefore contains the following major components. Chapter 1 is an introduction, containing background information about San Antonio Ranch, San Antonio New Town, and the HUD New Communities Program. Chapter 2 gives the long and involved history of the

SAR project from inception through litigation. In Chapter 3 the SAR events, issues, and actors are analyzed for their significance in local, regional, state, and federal politics. Finally, the implications of the SAR experience for new community development and policy in the United States are examined in Chapter 4. Although the study as outlined above is broad and ambitious, it does not purport to go beyond an evaluation of SAR and its meaning for the political and new community development context in which it exists.

The methodology employed in the research on the study included the following:

(a) carefully scrutinizing all available reports, correspondence, and records of the various events and facets of SAR

(b) conducting a total of 35 formal personal interviews (and many other informal interviews) with actors involved in, or knowledgeable concerning, one or more aspects of SAR and new communities in general

(c) searching thoroughly the literature of political science and government, with a particular focus on community power, decision making, intergovernmental relations, state politics, the federal bureaucracy, federal program impacts, and the politics of the environment and

(d) examining the extensive literature and other source materials on new communities, in particular Title VII new communities, and the processes by which they are developed.

From this research, over a period of many months, a picture of the SAR case gradually emerged, and could be related to a wider framework of government, politics, and new communities. In the Appendix there are listings of documents, literature, and interviewees consulted in the course of the research.

It should be noted here that some difficulties were encountered in obtaining materials and information regarding the SAR project. Presumably due to the sensitivity of the subject in San Antonio, some potential interviews were thwarted by the continuing "unavailability" of key participants, and some critical documents were "not for public viewing." Even at the U.S. Department of Housing and Urban Development (HUD), at least nominally subject to provisions of the Freedom of Information Act, some byzantine bureaucratic procedures effectively barred access to theoretically obtainable documents. The fact that these difficulties were encountered during the research for this study has certain connotations for the subject of the inquiry, and was treated accordingly.

A final prefatory note is also appropriate. The study and the conclusions are totally the products and responsibilities of the authors. The only assistance sought or received was through interviews and informal discussions with persons knowledgeable concerning

SAR, and through the project monitoring of the Political Science Department of St. Mary's University, under a grant from which the study was initiated. This study therefore represents independent, impartial research and analysis and is not connected with any factious activity or ulterior motives. It is an academic and journalistic endeavor and purports to be nothing else.

# CONTENTS

# LIST OF ACRONYMS

| | |
|---|---|
| AACOG | Alamo Area Council of Governments |
| CBE | Citizens for a Better Environment |
| CDC | Community Development Corporation (HUD) |
| CEQ | Council on Environmental Quality |
| CESO | Office of Community and Environmental Standards (HUD) |
| CMH | Christian, Miller, and Honts, Inc. |
| CORE | Congress of Racial Equality |
| CPSB | City of San Antonio Public Service Board |
| CWB | City of San Antonio Water Board |
| EIS | Environmental Impact Statement |
| EPA | U.S. Environmental Protection Agency |
| ETJ | Extraterritorial Jurisdiction |
| EUWD | Edwards Underground Water District |
| GARC | Government Application Review Committee (AACOG) |
| GGL | Good Government League |
| HUD | U.S. Department of Housing and Urban Development |
| MUD | Municipal Utility District |
| NDP | Neighborhood Development Program |
| NEPA | National Environmental Policy Act of 1969 |
| ONCD | Office of New Communities Development (HUD) |
| SADA | San Antonio Development Agency (Urban Renewal Agency) |
| SANT | San Antonio New Town (new town in-town) |
| SAR | San Antonio Ranch New Town |
| SARA | San Antonio River Authority |
| TWQB | Texas Water Quality Board |
| TWRC | Texas Water Rights Commission |
| UTSA | University of Texas at San Antonio |
| WQARB | Water Quality Advisory Review Board |

# The Politics of
# New Communities

## San Antonio Ranch Location Map
## Bexar County, Texas

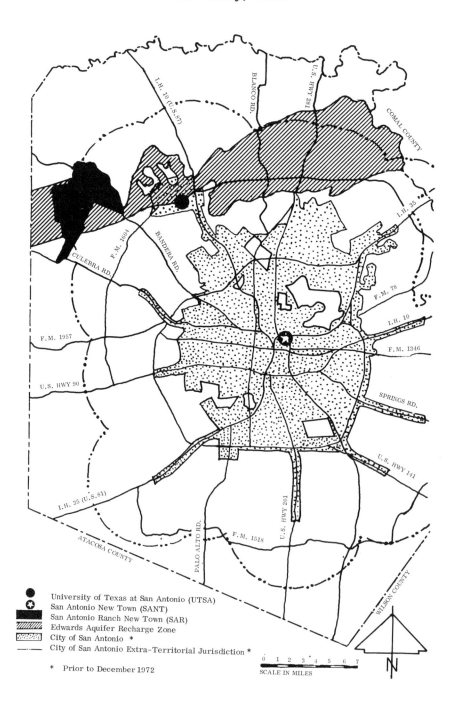

University of Texas at San Antonio (UTSA)
San Antonio New Town (SANT)
San Antonio Ranch New Town (SAR)
Edwards Aquifer Recharge Zone
City of San Antonio *
City of San Antonio Extra-Territorial Jurisdiction *

*   Prior to December 1972

0  1  2  3  4  5  6  7
SCALE IN MILES

N

## SAN ANTONIO RANCH

The proposed San Antonio Ranch New Town (SAR) is a preplanned, multiuse land development of 9,318 acres located in northwestern Bexar County, Texas, approximately 20 miles northwest of downtown San Antonio. The SAR development team, headed by the landowners and the firm of Christian, Miller, and Honts (CMH) of Austin, applied for and, on February 23, 1972, received an offer of commitment of an $18 million loan guarantee from the U.S. Department of Housing and Urban Development (HUD) under Title VII of the Housing and Urban Development Act of 1970. This action was conditional, pending further scientific studies concerning environmental impact, but impelled four local citizens' groups and two governmental entities to file a suit in federal district court to block implementation of SAR.

The SAR site is generally rolling and rocky, and lies directly over a portion of the Edwards Underground Aquifer, a large subsurface reservoir that provides almost all of San Antonio's water. Part of the site lies on direct recharge areas for the aquifer—porous limestone and geological faults through which precipitation and surface waters reach the aquifer. The site is located near the new University of Texas at San Antonio (UTSA) and the South Texas Medical Center.

SAR plans call for a 30-year development period, from 1974 to 2003. The ultimate population is projected to be 87,972. The developers plan a full range of land uses, including residential, commercial, office, industrial, open space/recreational, and public facilities. A total of 17,660 jobs are to be provided by the employment opportunities at SAR, including all occupational levels. There is planned a

1

wide variety of housing types in terms of density, sales/rental mix, and price range, including 25 percent subsidized units. Plans include a special mass-transit link between the SAR town center and downtown San Antonio (with no firm funding commitments) as well as internal circulation, including a continuous greenway system within the site's canyon network.

The SAR site is entirely outside of the corporate limits of any municipality, but, as of April 1974 the full 100 percent of it (58 percent prior to that date, 35 percent prior to December 1972) lies within the extraterritorial jurisdiction (ETJ) of the City of San Antonio. San Antonio consequently has subdivision platting approval authority, as well as power over annexation and incorporation, for the entire SAR site. Also, San Antonio in many cases provides utility services (electricity, gas, water, sewer) to the area in which SAR is located. Schools in the area are a function of the Northside Independent School District. Bexar County, on the other hand, provides few services and has almost no powers of land use control.

Three different and overlapping modes of governance have been proposed for SAR—a municipal utility district (MUD), annexation by the City of San Antonio, and a local citizens association. The MUD, approved in December 1973, by the Texas Water Rights Commission (TWRC), covers 3,166 acres (the earliest stages of development) and, through a board of directors appointed by the developers, has authorized the issuance of $26.9 million in bonds to finance infrastructure costs. The bonds will be a taxable obligation of all property owners within the MUD—included in any annexation by the City. The City Council of San Antonio, in a resolution in February 1972, expressed its intent to annex SAR at an appropriate time in the future. In a related contractual (nonbinding) agreement with SAR, the Council promised to supply utilities to SAR even if not annexed. In April 1974 the City Council, acting on an SAR petition, extended its ETJ to encompass the totality of the SAR site. The formation and role of the proposed citizens association has not yet been spelled out in detail.

The Edwards Aquifer extends west-to-east through six counties, from Brackettville to Kyle. The direct recharge zone of the aquifer covers some 100 square miles of Bexar County, along the northern edge of San Antonio, and was less than one percent developed as of 1972. The few legal restrictions on development over the recharge zone that were in existence at the time of the SAR approvals were embodied in a 1970 Edwards Order of the Texas Water Quality Board (TWQB), and chiefly concerned densities and permits for septic tanks. Largely due to SAR, the TWQB issued an amended Edwards Order in 1974, which extended controls to private sewage systems and set standards for effluent discharges within the recharge zone. Other public agencies in the region charged with ensuring the quality of water resources include the Edwards Underground Water District (EUWD) and the San Antonio River Authority (SARA).

## SAN ANTONIO NEW TOWN

The "other" new community in the SAR saga was San Antonio New Town (SANT), a proposed new town in-town near the center of San Antonio. Conceived in November 1971, during the peak of the SAR controversy, SANT surfaced publicly in June 1972, under almost the same development team as SAR, again headed by CMH, but including some San Antonio businessmen. It was to be a true public-private venture, combining private entrepreneurship and HUD Title VII sponsorship with public urban renewal powers for land acquisition, development, and write-down.

The SANT site was to consist of 558 acres in the northern portion of the San Antonio Central Business District. Plans included a town center and two residential neighborhoods, with an ultimate population after the 20-year development period of 19,415. Almost half of the housing units were planned to be subsidized.

Because of the overlapping sponsorship, a paired management approach between SANT and SAR was proposed. In addition, there were to be shared community facilities, a possible rapid-transit link, and complementary economic activities for the two new communities. SANT was to be the urban counterweight to the suburban SAR, and HUD officials were quite enthusiastic about this new community pairing experiment.

In early 1973, after achieving top priority status from HUD, the proposed new town in-town was debated and finally approved by the San Antonio City Council. However, a special bill introduced into the Texas legislature to amend Texas urban renewal law to permit non-competitive redevelopment—essential to SANT's existence—failed of passage in June 1973. HUD then removed SANT from its list of active projects and the $20 million loan guarantees were never awarded.

## THE NEW COMMUNITIES PROGRAM

Title VII of the Housing and Urban Development Act of 1970 declared a national urban growth policy and included an expanded New Communities Program as an instrument of that policy. The program, originally established under Title IV of the HUD Act of 1968, is designed to [encourage] the orderly development of well-planned, diversified, and economically sound new communities . . . [relying] to the maximum extent on private enterprise; strengthen the capacity of State and local governments to deal with local problems; preserve and enhance both the natural and urban environment; increase for all persons, particularly members of minority groups, the available choices of locations for living and working . . .; encourage the fullest utilization of the economic potential of older central cities, smaller towns, and rural communities; assist in the efficient production of a steady supply of residential, commercial, and industrial building sites at reasonable cost; increase the capability of all segments of the home-building industry . . . to utilize improved technology in producing the large volume of well-designed, inexpensive housing needed to accommodate population growth; help create neighborhoods designed for easier access between the places where people live and the places where they work and find recreation; . . . encourage desirable innovation in meeting domestic problems whether physical, economic, or social; . . . [and] improve the organizational capacity of the Federal Government to carry out programs of assistance for the development of new communities and the revitalization of the Nation's urban areas.[1]

To aid in achieving these objectives, federal guarantees of debt obligations of new community developers are available to assist in financing land acquisition and development and in constructing public facilities. In addition, the Act provided for supplementary grants up to 20 percent of project costs to state and local governments for certain types of federal public facilities projects in new communities. Eligible projects included transportation, health, education, recreation, open space, and water and sewer facilities. Other additional provisions of the Act included loans, technical assistance, and planning grants for new community developers. New communities were also to have a reserved pool of subsidized housing program funds. Most of the Act's provisions have never been implemented with congressional appropriations, and supplementary grants were terminated with the general HUD program freeze in July 1973. The latter, except for housing, have been partially reinstituted through the Secretary's discretionary fund authorized by the Housing and Community Development Act of 1974, for which new communities are eligible.

Four basic types of new communities have been identified for which Title VII assistance may be applied:

1. Satellite—economically balanced new communities within metropolitan areas, representing effective alternatives to urban sprawl

2. Add-on—additions to existing small towns and cities capable of conversion to growth centers

3. New towns in-town—compact subcities within or adjacent to existing cities which can assist the renewal of central cities and

4. Free-standing—frontier new communities distant from urban areas, heterogeneous and economically self-sufficient new towns to accommodate population growth

A fifth category was added in 1972; paired new communities—either satellite or in-town developments linked together in management, services, and transportation.[2] Of the 17 new communities approved for federal loan guarantees to date, all but three are satellite communities.

The program has been administered by the Office of New Communities Development (ONCD) in HUD, now called the New Communities Administration. Prior to any new community assistance, the ONCD (together with other HUD offices) conducts a thorough review of proposed project plans to ensure compliance with statutory and regulatory requirements. A favorable review culminates in official approval by the Board of Directors of the Community Development Corporation (CDC) within HUD (five members appointed by the president and the secretary). The Offer of Commitment is then made to the developer of the new community, usually with a specific guarantee ceiling amount. After official acceptance by the developer of the Offer, the terms and conditions under which both HUD and the developer must operate are negotiated and set forth in a Project Agreement, including a General Development Plan and Trust Indenture, both legal and binding for all parties.

San Antonio Ranch was the eighth new community of the seventeen approved to date by HUD under the New Communities Program. The entire group of approved Title VII communities is presented below, with the location, date of approval, and amount of loans guaranteed.

The total thus far approved falls far short of the original ONCD target of ten per year, and does not even approach the limits of guarantee commitments of $500 million imposed by the Act. No new communities at all were approved during 1974, and by the end of the year a moratorium had been declared by HUD on all new applications and approvals under the Title VII program, pending a complete re-evaluation of the program. Many studies of the New Communities Program have been commissioned, and congressional hearings are scheduled on the subject. In the aggregate, the recession of 1974, high interest rates, energy uncertainties, and inflation of costs have endangered most large-scale real estate developments, at the same

TABLE 1

Title VII New Communities[3]

| Name | State | General Location | Date of Offer | Amount of Guarantee |
|---|---|---|---|---|
| 1. Jonathan | Minnesota | near Minneapolis | 2/70 | $21,000,000 |
| 2. St. Charles Comm. | Maryland | near Wash., D.C. | 6/70 | 24,000,000 |
| 3. Park Forest South | Illinois | near Chicago | 6/70 | 30,000,000 |
| 4. Flower Mound | Texas | bet. Dallas/Fort Worth | 12/70 | 18,000,000 |
| 5. Maumelle | Arkansas | near Little Rock | 12/70 | 7,500,000 |
| 6. Cedar-Riverside | Minnesota | in Minneapolis | 6/71 | 24,000,000 |
| 7. Riverton | New York | near Rochester | 12/71 | 12,000,000 |
| 8. San Antonio Ranch | Texas | near San Antonio | 2/72 | 18,000,000 |
| 9. The Woodlands | Texas | near Houston | 3/72 | 50,000,000 |
| 10. Granada | New York | near Rochester | 4/72 | 22,000,000 |
| 11. Soul City | North Carolina | north of Raleigh–Durham | 6/72 | 14,000,000 |
| 12. Radisson[a] | New York | near Syracuse | 6/72 | c |
| 13. Harbison | South Carolina | near Columbia | 10/72 | 13,000,000 |
| 14. Roosevelt Island[b] | New York | in New York | 12/72 | c |
| 15. Shenandoah | Georgia | near Atlanta | 2/73 | 40,000,000 |
| 16. Newfields | Ohio | near Dayton | 10/73 | 32,000,000 |
| 17. Beckett | New Jersey | near Philadelphia | 10/73 | d |

[a]Formerly Lysander.
[b]Formerly Welfare Island.
[c]Projects of New York State Urban Development Corp.—eligible for grant assistance but not loan guarantees.
[d]Offer of loan guarantees and assistance not accepted by developer.

time demonstrating severe financial weaknesses in several Title VII new communities—a situation which has led to some renegotiation of loan guarantee amounts. Title VII developers, on the other hand, organized as the League of New Community Developers, have blamed HUD for their problems—the ever-increasing guidelines, scrutiny, and time delays involved in the application process, as well as unfulfilled promises for supplementary grants and other assistance.

All in all, the future of the New Communities Program is quite clouded at this point. By way of documenting the short history of the program, Chapter 2 presents the illustrative study of the dynamics of the program as it operated for the San Antonio Ranch.

## NOTES

1. Housing and Urban Development Act of 1970, P. L. 91-609, Title VII, Sec. 710(f); 42 U.S.C. 4511(f).

2. HUD Draft Regulations: Assistance for New Communities (Urban Growth and New Community Development Act of 1970), 24 CFR 720 (August 7, 1972), Sec. 720.6(b).

3. Source of information was the Department of Housing and Urban Development.

# 2

# A CASE HISTORY OF
# SAN ANTONIO RANCH

EARLY PERIOD

Land Acquisition

The story of San Antonio Ranch New Town began back in May 1965, when Hayden W. Head, a Corpus Christi attorney also "involved in ranching, farming, and general investment," vice-chairman of the Coastal Bend Council of Governments and a member of the University of Texas Development Board, took an option on 8,236.15 acres of northwest Bexar County land owned by William J. Lytle, Jr., partly in estate of his parents. Actually, in the original option agreement, Head was accompanied by partners Leonard C. Traylor and A.J. Lindsay, each with a one-third interest. The price for the land was to be $165 an acre, according to the option agreement which after extension ultimately ran for 2 1/2 years and payments for which totaled $30,500 (applicable to the sale price).

The motivation of the group apparently was speculative in nature, probably for development potential of this large parcel of land, but also perhaps with a view to a site for a new university in the state system, which at that time was not public knowledge. In any event, prior to the exercise of the option on December 29, 1967, Head bought out Lindsay's one-third share and about half of Traylor's one-third share of the option, at prorated portions of the total $30,500. The purchase of the land itself cost $1,306,701.07 (after deduction of option payments and certain other items), and all but $100,000 was paid in cash. The remainder was held in escrow account pending a resurvey of the land at Head's expense. The resurvey finally added 112 acres to the total.

The purchase of the Lytle Ranch was accompanied by a grazing lease on the land to R. G. Pope. The lease ran for many years and became a sore point to Head, who sued Pope in June 1968 for release of the land from the lease incrementally. The suit was settled out of court in August, with the purchase of the lease on 1,000 acres and an option to purchase the balance of it at any time. This option was exercised in January 1969.

During 1968 there were many nominal alterations in the land ownership, chiefly because of the delicate financial arrangements that had been made to pay cash for the purchase. Traylor ceded his claim to 914 acres to Head in exchange for the assumption of two promissory notes. Ed Lowrance became the owner of 644 acres, and Head granted one-half interest in his remaining 7,704 acres to his stepson, Randolph Farenthold (who died in 1972), presumably for financial reasons. Finally, in June 1968 Head and Farenthold claimed the name San Antonio Ranch for their land holdings and set up business.

The tenuous financial balance was again underscored in 1969 with the transfer by Head and Farenthold of their 7,704 acres into family trusts, the five Lambert trusts, bringing chief administrators (and beneficiaries) J. Lawrence Wood and Richard L. Wood into the SAR picture. The trusts then assumed some $760,413 in outstanding notes.[1]

Thus by June 1969 the land was in solid ownership, the debts under control, and the principal landowners assembled and presumably thinking quite alike. In addition, the early idea of SAR as a site for the university had germinated and was ready to be acted upon.

The UTSA Site Location Decision

It had been clear in early 1967 that there would be a new state university in San Antonio some time in the future. A bill of authorization had been introduced into the legislature but failed of passage, largely due to poor timing politically. During 1968 several offers of land for a university site were made, including one of 400 acres from the giant Southwest Research Institute property on the western edge of San Antonio. It was generally conceded that the legislature would pass a bill authorizing such a university, although there was disagreement as to whether the university should be part of the University of Texas system. As finally authorized officially on September 1, 1969, the University of Texas at San Antonio was born within that system, thus falling under the jurisdiction of the University's Board of Regents in policy matters.

The regents began their site selection duties in June 1969, even before the authorization bill had been passed by the Senate. Apparently, there was never any question in their minds that the site would be donated; no provision was made at any point for purchase of land. This approach to site selection naturally provoked a flurry of land speculation and politicking by many real estate operators who understood the magnificent opportunities that would be available in the vicinity of the UTSA site.

It was also in June 1969 that San Antonio Ranch was ready to move toward fulfilling development objectives (with the concomitant land value appreciation). Head had been aiming for the UTSA sweepstakes for a long time, and by June the race was on. He commissioned William L. Pereira Associates for planning and design of a San Antonio Ranch university community. The Pereira firm, a well-known Los Angeles architectural and planning group, was particularly suited for the assignment, both technically and reputationally, because of its well-received design work on the Irvine Ranch in California. Irvine is an 88,000-acre property which is in the early stages of development into a new city, the first community of which was University Park, whose focus is a new campus of the University of California. With a good master plan, and a large site already in hand, it was not unreasonable of Head to believe that his Ranch could be put across as the UTSA location.

Later in 1969 Head brought in the firm of Christian, Miller, and Honts (CMH) of Austin to put together, manage, and promote the SAR package. George Christian, an aide to former President Lyndon B. Johnson, had resigned to return to Austin to open a political affairs and public relations firm. Robert G. (Bob) Honts, a young San Antonian with experience in business and governmental affairs, joined Christian and extended the CMH operations to the field of packaging program applications for cities. This component of the business had become involved in the Flower Mound New Town between Dallas and Fort Worth, through Honts' connections with Edward S. Marcus, the developer. The CMH work on Flower Mound was successful both in management and in governmental relations in Washington. The CMH record there came to Head's attention, and the firm was made a partner in the San Antonio Ranch venture.

The SAR business that Head and Farenthold had created in 1968 was by now a limited partnership for real estate investment. An entity called New Town Management, Inc., was the general partner and thus the active agent. In effect, this was CMH. The landowners— Head, Farenthold, Lowrance, and the Lambert trusts—were limited partners with pro-rata shares. Other investors were actively sought, since the initial capital requirements were inevitably high in any large-scale new community development. Among the investors were CMH contacts Mack Fleming of Austin, Robert B. Russell of Charleston, South Carolina, William L. Gunter of Atlanta, Georgia, and William O. Rothwell of Dallas.

Honts brought to SAR the idea of utilizing the federal loan guarantees for new communities available under the then current Title IV of the HUD Act of 1968, for which Flower Mound was in the process of applying. The concept of a Title IV new community centered around a new state university was indeed attractive to Head, his partners, and officials in the Office of New Communities Development (ONCD) at HUD, with whom preliminary consultations were held. Furthermore, only minor alterations in the Pereira work already underway would be required.

By the end of 1969, when the concept of a Title IV university new community was being developed, what was needed for SAR was some lobbying of the Board of Regents in favor of the SAR site. Already other operators were putting together sites and political influence packages in order to win the competition. Although there was a University committee to review and evaluate alternative sites, the dominant view was that the unpredictable regents would be considering a mostly different set of criteria. Head's competition in the UTSA sweepstakes included Bexar County commissioners, Southwest Research Institute, a real estate investor linked with former Governor John B. Connally, several civic leaders pushing HemisFair Plaza (site of the 1968 HemisFair World's Fair) in downtown San Antonio, and some seven others located outside of San Antonio in every direction. Head could count on the efforts of George Christian with various contacts on the state level, including his former boss Connally, and on his own relationships with the University policy makers and other politicians, including Senator John B. Tower.

By early 1970 Honts was busy assembling a team of consultants for the new community. With favorable initial readings from HUD (in February), the next step was the Pre-Application. This was submitted in March 1970 with the assistance of Pereira, Rothwell, and Gladstone Associates of Washington, D. C., highly regarded economic consultants also veterans of Flower Mound, as well as Head's Corpus Christi law firm, Head and Kendrick. The Pre-Application is a small set of documents outlining the basic characteristics of the project, a rough concept plan, a generalized description of how the new community will participate in its region's expected growth, and other related matters. It enables HUD to acknowledge formally a project's status and to establish its priority relative to other pending applications. For SAR, the Pre-Application was submitted as a university-centered new community, obviously prematurely, but in the hope of the self-fulfilling prophecy—that HUD's blessing would solidify SAR as the regents' choice.

After acceptance of the Pre-Application by ONCD in HUD and the issuance of a letter inviting a Final Application, the UTSA site selection process came to a climax. In a Board of Regents meeting in

11

El Paso on May 29, 1970, a site was approved for UTSA near the intersection of I-10 and F.M. 1604, some six miles from SAR. The selected site of 600 acres was to be donated by Mary Ann Smothers Bruni, Charles A. Kuper, and Servtex Materials Company, subject to meeting certain title and accessibility conditions. The selection was a setback to Head, who had appeared at the final meeting to increase the SAR offer to 1,500 acres. His political clout had evidently fallen short. [2]

## Change of Concept

The UTSA site decision, while ironically insuring a considerable appreciation of land value on SAR due to proximity, caused a great deal of uncertainty regarding the Title IV new community concept approved so far by HUD. The acceptance of the Pre-Application had been based on SAR as a unique university new community, which HUD wanted very much. Without this underpinning, SAR was a marginal project compared with its competition nationwide. Finally, HUD agreed that the concept could be reworked and an amended Pre-Application submitted. This time the focus was on a technical center for skill training which would serve, among others, the Mexican-American population which constitutes half of the San Antonio area total. As such, SAR would again be a unique project for ONCD, and thus justify renewed top priority consideration.

Consequently, the SAR Pre-Application was quickly adjusted to reflect the new focus and resubmitted to ONCD. The signal was again given to proceed on the Final Application. The Final Application for a new community is a substantial set of documents, the basic components of which are a development plan, market analysis, financial analysis, environmental statement, social analysis, land appraisal, financial statements, fiscal impact analysis, and miscellaneous items relating to the sponsor and his intentions. In order to prepare the Final Application, Honts had to assemble a sizable team of consultants, including, in addition to Pereira, Gladstone, Rothwell, and Head & Kendrick, already involved: Marvin Shipman, San Antonio, engineering; Dr. George Kozmetsky, Austin, business and industrial development; and Rowsey and Rowsey, San Antonio, and Charles H. Noble, San Antonio, appraisal.

The CMH-directed consultant team completed the Final Application for submittal to ONCD on November 12, 1970. Up to this point almost no interaction had taken place between the development team and the local and regional governments in the San Antonio area. The only notification of the project's existence prior to the submittal of the Final Application was on October 13, 1970, to the Alamo Area Council of Governments (AACOG) Regional Planning Division, although AACOG had already been aware of SAR for several months through ONCD in HUD. At about the same time, Governor Preston Smith's Division of Planning Coordination was likewise informed. Although Title IV required governmental approvals, the SAR approach was within the letter of the regulations in initiating such action at the same time as submitting the Final Application.

## GOVERNMENTAL RELATIONS PERIOD

### The A-95 Review

After the submittal to ONCD, a new phase began for SAR—presentations to and endorsements from a myriad of public agencies even marginally to be affected by SAR. First was a November 23, 1970, presentation at AACOG of the concept only. Approximately thirty persons representing city and county agencies were in attendance, and apparently received the concept without any undue excitement. Later, after official request, the SAR project was scheduled for official action by the AACOG Government Application Review Committee (GARC) for March 16, 1971. This action was required under the A-95 authority possessed by the AACOG as regional clearinghouse for governmental actions.[3]

As of the March 16 meeting, SAR developers had sought and obtained only the endorsement of the Texas Water Quality Board (TWQB) and the Governor's Division of Planning Coordination, plus another from Blair Reeves, Bexar county judge, read during the meeting. Because of the limited promulgation of the SAR plans, very few people in the area were even aware of the existence of the project, much less its magnitude and implications.

At that time the AACOG GARC membership included a cross section of professionals from the public and private sectors. Among others, several architects, an environmentalist, heads of some City of San Antonio departments (Planning, Public Works, and Parks and Recreation), and a city councilman were members of the GARC. Curiously, Bob Honts did not attend the March 16 meeting to conduct the presentation. SAR developers were bombarded with questions about the plan, the environmental impact, economic feasibility, social planning, and governmental impacts. A HUD San Antonio Area Office official claimed to have learned of the project only a few days earlier, noting the tight control maintained by ONCD in Washington on the New

Communities Program. Finally, the developers were asked to prepare a full response to the questions raised, for a full project review at the next regularly scheduled GARC meeting on April 20.

Honts stepped up the pace of activity during the intervening month. He obtained endorsements from the UTSA and San Antonio Junior College District, and the superintendent of the Northside Independent School District, and an agreement for provision of water to SAR from the City of San Antonio Water Board (CWB). A full report was prepared by CMH for the GARC members, rebutting all questions raised and presenting much more detail on the SAR project. The meeting itself brought out almost twice the number of interested persons than had the previous one, including Bob Honts, Hayden Head, William L. Pereira, and Jack A. Underhill (deputy director of ONCD). Char White, President of the Citizens for a Better Environment (CBE), took the offensive in denigrating the environmental impact analysis carried out by CMH as superficial. Hugh C. Yantis, Jr., Executive Director of the TWQB, who had already endorsed the project, declared that the effect of SAR on the Edwards Aquifer would be negligible. Yantis' presence at the meeting was something of a sensation, since up to that time he had consistently declined invitations to attend AACOG meetings on water quality and refused to become involved in Edwards Aquifer problems. His old business associate Hayden Head and GARC member Gilbert Garza had persuaded him to testify at this meeting. A battle of motions to approve and disapprove SAR's application led to another postponement, this time until a special meeting on May 11, 1971.

Thus up to this point the only strident opposition voice was that of Char White. Curiously, the City of San Antonio had offered up only two questions—on annexation and the allocation of federal funds—both from City Manager Gerald C. Henckel's office. The progress of SAR was being hindered, but clearly no stampede was occurring. Some groups and individuals with a potential interest at stake, such as the Edwards Underground Water District and the Urban Renewal Agency of San Antonio, failed to attend the meetings after repeated invitations. The City Planning Department was in the process of seeking a new director. Some observers have attributed the general blase attitude to ignorance; most people thought it was merely another big subdivision. The A-95 review process, the formal and legal mechanism for governmental and citizen review of proposed developments, was a wonderful opportunity for comment and opposition, but virtually no one was interested enough to bother.

Prior to the May 11 special GARC meeting, Honts contacted all GARC members with a letter which promised studies and technological precautions to prevent pollution to the aquifer, in an effort to allay fears of the unknown and to soften any potential opposition.

There were meetings with City Manager Henckel and with Parks and Recreation Department officials, with AACOG regional planners, and with the City of San Antonio Public Service Board (CPSB) staff, out of which came an agreement to provide electricity and gas to the SAR site. On the other side, the potential opposition forces were unable to launch a significant counteroffensive. The several environmentalist groups had been actively preoccupied in battling the San Antonio North Expressway and failed to perceive in SAR an issue of equal importance. In addition, their finances and volunteer support were flagging at the time. Even the lone voice of environmental preservation, that of CBE President White, was diminished by persuasion from Honts and a promise of an advisory board on aquifer water quality problems (after an abortive attempt to influence her through her husband's superior in his educational television job).

The May 11 GARC meeting itself, attended by a large but less imposing crowd than its predecessor, was brief and to the point regarding SAR. It was given favorable review by unanimous vote (four abstentions), but with two recommendations: that environmental impact studies be carried out, and that the sanitary sewers be connected to the San Antonio regional system. The next day the AACOG Executive Committee on a motion by Judge Reeves also approved the SAR project, and with the same two recommendations. The composition of the Executive Committee of AACOG is political (versus the professional GARC) and is representative of a broad cross section of the region's elected officials. Its action had the effect of closing the A-95 review process on SAR and forwarding the required regional and local approval to ONCD in Washington. As far as CMH and ONCD officials were concerned, the governmental review phase of SAR was finished.

## HUD's Application Review

The month of May 1971 was also critical in terms of the application review process for SAR taking place in Washington concurrent with the A-95 review. Initial staff reactions to the Final Application had been mixed: the SAR was referred to as a "retread," reflecting the alterations made subsequent to the UTSA decision. It was viewed as a mediocre project, and the ONCD staff was interested chiefly in skimming the cream of the crop of applications (which was quite large at the time).

However, there were several mitigating circumstances in the case of SAR. For one thing, Honts and his consultants were booming SAR as the one project then alive in the country that would benefit a

Mexican-American population. The changes from the university focus had included a proposal for a technical center which would provide training for low-skill persons in conjunction with SAR industries. The intention was to attract potential workers, primarily Mexican-Americans, from the inner city of San Antonio to live and/or to work at SAR. The concept was not backed up by commitments for funding.

The minority group focus for new communities was actively being solicited by HUD Assistant Secretary Samuel C. Jackson, who as general manager of the CDC was in charge of the New Communities Program. Through his support, the marginal new community application of St. Charles Communities in Maryland was approved, over some amount of staff dissent, chiefly due to its objective of building 80 percent of its housing units for low and moderate income persons. Similarly, the relatively weak proposal of former CORE director Floyd B. McKissick for Soul City in North Carolina was being reworked and improved with ONCD staff cooperation, in order to bring it to acceptable standards for project approval. SAR was seen as falling into the same category.

Secondly, and somewhat ironically, the existence of the Edwards Aquifer underlaying SAR presented something of a challenge to the ONCD staff. No other new community already approved or in review provided the opportunity to prove that technology could solve environmental problems. In essence, SAR would become a model of an environmentally perfect new community—the ultimate in ecology. The challenge of the aquifer was not as strong a positive factor as the Mexican-American link, but it helped to increase staff enthusiasm for the project.

A final and most important circumstance bearing on the SAR review was an unusually strong level of political support for the project. Political pressure of varying degrees is pro forma for the federal bureaucratic project review process in all departments, and had become so during the short lifetime of the ONCD. One HUD official declared that "any new community which doesn't have the support of both the representatives and the senators of the state is dead." It is not unusual to expect that new community developers, generally large firms or wealthy individuals, would have access to and would utilize political resources that would have an impact on the HUD review and decision-making process.

In the case of SAR, the development team was blessed with stronger than usual political connections. George Christian, CMH principal, was former President Johnson's press secretary, and a close associate of then Treasury Secretary John Connally. Connally himself was reputed to have a direct interest in SAR as an investor (though this has been denied). Hayden Head had been a friend of Senator John Tower for many years, as Republicans in Democratic

Texas. Suffice it to conclude here that the SAR project had a great deal of potential political resources and evidently used them to advantage. Not only was HUD giving the SAR application every chance of meeting review standards, but the process was speeded up considerably with the pressure from above, through Jackson's office.

By May 1971 the ONCD review staff was demanding answers to many questions raised, and that certain features of the proposed project be altered. As a result, an actually revised Final Application was submitted May 13, 1971, with related materials still straggling in as late as the end of that month. The major changes in the project proposal involved (1) the acquisition of some 970 acres of additional land, chiefly along the Bandera Road frontage, intended to forestall parasitical development nearby (2) an increase in the programmed allocation of low and moderate income housing units over the life of the project, and (3) an increase in the development period from twenty to thirty years to accord with ONCD's views of the market absorption potentials. A large amount of additional documentation was requested from the developers. This included applicable laws and regulations on water quality, subdivision platting, water provision, and building and plumbing codes; revised cash-flow analysis taking account of the longer development period, without assuming a maximum of federal categorical grants, and with an assumption of a lower level of industrial and research and development site sales; and various further explications of governance, transportation, infrastructure costs, development organization, and projected sales paces for industry and low and moderate housing.

In the months subsequent to the May revisions, the ONCD staff satisfied itself that the SAR project was sound enough to be submitted to the Board of Directors of the CDC for approval. This was done first through an August 25 report from Assistant Secretary Jackson to the CDC on SAR, and then at a full presentation to the Board on September 15. The one additional requirement prior to approval was the preparation of an Environmental Impact Statement (EIS) for SAR, as HUD had determined to be necessary in this case. (HUD now requires an EIS for all Title VII new communities as major federal project actions.) According to the National Environmental Policy Act of 1969 (NEPA), an EIS is to be prepared by federal agencies, but the New Communities Program is unusual in that the private developer is the source of the initiative, the planning, and the execution of the project. Thus HUD interpreted that the developer should provide all the information for the EIS, and ONCD would write the EIS. [4] As might be expected, the SAR developer ended up preparing the entire EIS in order to save ONCD the staff effort and to depict the project in the most favorable possible light. CMH was aware of the potential for opposition on environmental grounds and thus was

interested in proceeding through the EIS phase with caution. Full
developer preparation of the EIS was of questionable legality under
NEPA, but HUD would never admit that this had in fact been the case.
Perhaps such preparation was understandable in this project, due to
the complexities of the plan and the environmental problems and
remedies, but it contravened the letter and intent of NEPA.

The Draft EIS was published on September 13, 1971, and sent
to thirteen public agencies, all federal except AACOG, for comments
within 30 days. The fact that all pertinent state, regional, and local
agencies, save AACOG, were excluded from the EIS process denotes
a significant failure on HUD's part. The Draft EIS itself was typed
in the recognizable CMH typewriter characters, with HUD's usual
type characters on the summary sheet and with "This Department"
inserted as a correction.

The Draft EIS content amounted to a whitewash of legitimate
environmental concerns. The aquifer was hardly mentioned; most
of the statement comprised a general description of the SAR plan.
The "adverse environmental effects" mentioned included noise, automobiles, and thermal emissions, the effects of which would be min-
imized through grading, bicycle paths, and greenbelts. Serious
problems such as sewage wastes were dismissed as already recognized and easily solvable. "Alternatives to the proposed action" were
treated in a cursory, one-page manner, and the "irreversible and
irretrievable commitments of resources" involved only the loss of
marginal grazing and farming land. Finally, the few endorsements
and agreements obtained by the developer to the time were displayed
as attachments to the Draft EIS.


San Antonio Says No


At the beginning of September 1971 Edward F. Davis became
Director of Planning for the City of San Antonio. Davis was an ardent
environmentalist, with a special concern about development on the
Edwards Aquifer, and a member of the CBE and the Area Policy
Council. With the publication of the Draft EIS, Davis felt that a significant oversight had been perpetrated by the SAR developers and
HUD in excluding the City of San Antonio from the list of agencies
from which comments on the Draft EIS were being solicited. He and
other environmentalists were distressed by the Draft EIS and its
summary dismissal of potential ill effects of SAR on the aquifer. He
was determined to use the Planning position to rectify the oversight.

Davis contacted the HUD San Antonio Area Office for an inclusion
of the City on the agency list. The Area Office, a party to none of the

EIS activity and to little of the new community process, finally referred him to the HUD Regional Office in Fort Worth. A Regional Office environmental officer, Otis M. Trimble, recently appointed to the position, decided that Davis (as staff to the Planning and Zoning Commission) should receive a copy. Trimble sent him an apologetic letter, dated October 6, which requested comments prior to the end of the 30-day period on October 13, and which implied an opportunity for a go/no-go position on the entire SAR project. For Davis, this opportunity was beyond his hopes, in being asked for comments with promised impact and in the short time frame available, which would preclude Honts from the chance for another sales pitch.

With concurrence of the city manager, Davis sent a letter dated October 12, 1971, to HUD in Washington requesting an extension until the next Planning Commission and City Council meetings and expressing concern over four aspects of SAR:

- conflict with other goals for San Antonio area
- storm drainage as a pollution threat to the aquifer
- impact on the surrounding area, and
- relationships between the City and SAR

At the regular meeting of the Planning Commission on October 20, 1971, the Commission unanimously endorsed the staff questions and urged the City Council to give a new town in-town priority over SAR. The Planning Commission, with a composition strongly laced with land developers and real estate operators, including Chairman M. M. (Mel) Hughes, was quite impressed with the Planning Department Staff evaluation of the impact SAR would have as competition with other developers' activities in the northwest San Antonio Area. The next day, at the regular City Council meeting, the council affirmed the Planning Commission action, and specifically took a no-go position on SAR. This decision was telegraphed to Assistant Secretary Jackson at HUD and confirmed in a letter from City Manager Henckel.

Although Jackson's supercilious response of a week later stated that HUD would act on SAR as it saw fit, in actuality HUD was shaken by this late blow. According to the statutes and regulations, the approval of the City of San Antonio was not required, since its opportunity to express its views was through its various representatives on the AACOG Executive Committee and GARC during the A-95 review process. Practically, however, no such project could be finally approved without the concurrence of the only major municipality in the area, which was to provide the water, gas, electricity, and sewer to the new community, which had subdivision platting authority over part of the site, and which was expected to annex the new community once developed. On the other hand, the SAR project had been in effect approved already by HUD, or else the Draft EIS would not have been prepared. HUD had gone too far with SAR to reverse itself, so the position of the city had to be changed.

Meanwhile, comments on the Draft EIS were pouring in to HUD from the solicited sources, as well as many unsolicited comments in addition. Most had much to add concerning potential environmental consequences of SAR, but most concluded with guardedly positive opinions that the developer would overcome any problems encountered. Such comments on the Draft EIS were intended to be rebutted point by point for the Final EIS. In mid-October the CDC met again on SAR and formally an offer of commitment would be made for SAR "at the appropriate time."

After the City Council action of October 21, Bob Honts became the focus of the developer attempt to reverse the tide of events. He set out to win over enough councilmen one by one. He prepared a special report for the council for use with his scheduled presentation at the council informal session on November 4. At that meeting, Honts offered a contract between SAR and the city to protect its interests and assistance on any new town in-town project the city might undertake, but the council refused to remove the no-go posture taken earlier, although various members expressed enthusiasm over the idea of the new town in-town along the San Antonio River. It became apparent that at least one councilman had already been won over—the powerful Charles L. Becker. Becker, president of Handy Andy food stores, was normally prodevelopment and growth, but had been stalled at the earlier meeting by the emphasis on the new town in-town. Becker expressed contempt for the contention that SAR could not avoid pollution of the aquifer. At least two other councilmen generally followed his lead on development matters, but they were holding firm until more information would be available on the new town in-town.

At this point the basic issues were bifurcated. The City Council did not oppose the SAR project on grounds of possible pollution to the aquifer; the council was officially concerned only with the potential for stripping the central city of federal funds. The new town in-town proposal was a vague concept promoted first as a symbol of the priorities of the central city over the suburban SAR. Proposals for a new town in-town, including one along the river, had been in existence for some time, but it now became a cause celebre for opposition to SAR. The negative action by City Council, whatever the issue involved, stimulated and opened the door for a multitude of other public agencies and private organizations to enter the fray on their own terms. None of the issues was new at this time, but Davis and the Planning Department staff articulated the full range of major issues when many actors were entering and thereby defined the scope of conflict. The two major issues around which most opposition clung were that of the aquifer and its pollution and that of federal funds for the central city versus SAR.

With the November 4 City Council meeting, the newspaper, television, and radio coverage really began in avalanche proportions. Up to that time there had been a few articles concerning SAR, especially back in May, but these were mainly informative and somewhat reverential descriptions of SAR and new community development. The no-go stance of City Council had likewise been reported in matter-of-fact terms. But immediately prior to the November 4 meeting, the San Antonio Express and to a lesser extent the News, both under the same ownership, began a daily outpouring of articles and editorials which more than any other single factor can be credited with broadening the conflict from City Council to the civic-minded portion of the city as a whole. From the point of view of the newspaper and its chief reportorial protagonist, Deborah Weser, the purpose was to ensure that the ultimate decision on SAR would be made openly and in light of as many relevant issues as possible. The barrage was maintained for over two weeks before pressure from Honts aimed directly at Weser through her superiors succeeded in curtailing the coverage. At about the same time, activity in the case was also slowing its pace. The television and radio stations devoted some coverage to the major events, but not with the consistency or the fervor of the Express and the News. The other major newspaper, the Light, was conspicuously lacking in its coverage of SAR in this period, except for perfunctory reporting of significant happenings at public meetings.

With the November 4 City Council meeting and the newspaper coverage of the SAR controversy, the scope of the conflict was enlarged rapidly as individuals and groups entered. Bexar County Judge Blair Reeves admitted second thoughts since his tentative endorsement of SAR in March, and advocated blocking the HUD funding, claiming concern for the aquifer water and federal funds allocations. County Commissioner A. J. Ploch almost succeeded in an attempt for an outright opposition to SAR from the Commissioners Court, but the court passed a resolution opposing in general any further development on the aquifer until studies could be conducted to prove that it would not be environmentally affected. The subject of SAR was revived in AACOG Executive Committee with the staff review comments for the Draft EIS, but the Committee voted to table rather than adopt the critical comments until city and county action would be completed. Thus the favorable review of May still stood.

The San Antonio River Authority became involved on the staff level with the opposition of Louis T. Rosenberg, but manager Fred Pfeiffer was not yet clear on the issues and was even quoted as favoring the SAR proposal. By mid-November, however, SARA was on record in opposition. Colonel McDonald Weinert, General Manager of the Edwards Underground Water District, who had endorsed SAR in May under pressure from Yantis, began to change his mind after learning more about the potential SAR hazards. He claimed that he had never even received a SAR Draft EIS. Private groups such as the CBE, the Sierra Club, and the League of Women Voters rallied to the opposition when SAR became a hot issue. Even U.S. Representative Henry B. Gonzalez took pains to deny that he was in favor of SAR or had ever heard of SAR, but also declined to involve himself further.

<br>

### The Moratorium


On November 11, 1971, Mayor John Gatti met with William J. Nicoson, Director of ONCD, in Washington to present the council's case against SAR and for a new town in-town. He had intended on meeting with Assistant Secretary Jackson, but was shunted aside to Nicoson, with Bob Honts in attendance. Gatti requested and was granted a 30- to-45 day moratorium on any HUD action with regard to SAR, as a "cooling off period" until City Council could study the matter more fully, and in order to make more concrete plans for a new town in-town.

The new town in-town idea had been floating around civic circles in San Antonio for a long time, ever since an abortive attempt in 1967-69 by HUD and the Urban Renewal Agency for a new town on surplus Fort Sam Houston property (finally smothered politically with the intervention of Gonzalez and the military).[5] Later, the river corridor seemed the logical place for a new town, and even CMH had discussed the possibility among themselves. But when Davis and the Planning Department were defining the issues involved in SAR in October, the inevitable link was made between the federal funding competition issue and a potential new town in-town. This particular issue was crucial in rallying important opposition elements, including Mayor Gatti, that were not convinced enough of the aquifer danger to stand firm on that alone. CMH and HUD likewise realized the potential in an actual new town in-town proposal for neutralizing much of the important opposition argument. Therefore at Jackson's suggestion Nicoson and the ONCD began to investigate new town in-town feasibility and to publicize their interest in one, as a means of breaking the logjam on SAR. Nicoson scheduled a visit to San Antonio on both projects for the City Council meeting of November 29.

The moratorium was a blessing for the SAR development team, which had been losing ground steadily in the fast pace of events of the past month. Even at the beginning of the moratorium more bad news arrived with the publication on November 16 of a Planning Department report prepared for the City Council claiming that SAR would cost the city some $5.7 million in the first decade of development, followed by a demand from AACOG Executive Director Al Notzon for an AACOG staff reappraisal of the SAR and new town in-town projects. The moratorium provided some respite from the daily events and an opportunity to operate as CMH knew best—dealing with each opponent and each issue individually and personally. And the scheduled November 29 council meeting provided a target date. The CMH strategy involved pressure on every major opponent, through employers, board members, or clients of each one, and supplemented by personal visits from Honts. In addition, CMH commissioned extensive further consultant work to counter the Planning Department report and other opposition arguments.

Each key opponent, including most of City Council members, was subjected to intense pressure during this two-week period. CMH would act through sympathetic persons a "couple of steps upstream" from the opponent. The nature of these relationships can be surmised at best: for Davis, some councilmen; for Pfeiffer and Weinert, their respective boards; for Councilman Gilbert Garza, his patron H.B. Zachry; for Councilman Carol Haberman, William Ochse, an associate of SAR developers and owner of the St. Anthony Hotel, which was managed by Haberman's husband; for Weser, Express-News publisher Charles O. Kilpatrick; for Urban Renewal Director Winston Martin, who had raised his voice in opposition, former Mayor Walter W. McAllister and members of his board. These pressures were supplemented by personal visits from Honts, accompanied by an appropriate proponent. Yantis and Honts talked to Pfeiffer and Weinert; Ochse and Honts to Davis, and so forth. Mayor Gatti received pressures and visits from many sources, including some top figures in the Good Government League and its roster of business and community leaders, among them Councilman Becker, Ochse, Honts associate B.J. McCombs, and San Antonio Light Publisher Frank Bennack (tied by kinship to SAR landowners). Some of the arguments raised in favor of SAR during these personal visits concerned benefits of SAR and reassurances against any possible negative effects; other lines were far more blunt:

If we don't get this, San Antonio won't get any more grants from HUD. . . . We've got it rigged, friend, and if you don't go along with this, San Antonio is going to be cut off. HUD wants this project. . . . we control the purse strings to San Antonio.

as reported by one of the recipients of such a Honts visit.

At the same time, technical arguments were also being refined and substantiated. As parts of a special report prepared for the City Council for the November 29 meeting, Honts hired three consultants to rebut major arguments of the SAR opposition. The three were (1) Dr. L. J. Turk, a University of Texas at Austin geologist, commenting on the potential pollution of the aquifer; (2) W. O. Rothwell, a limited partner in SAR and a CPA from Dallas, with a detailed fiscal impact study for the City of San Antonio, addressing the November 16 Planning Department report, and (3) Clark Rector, an Austin economic consultant, attempting to refute such charges against SAR as competition for federal funding with the inner city, uncontrollable induced development along the SAR periphery, and potential disqualification of San Antonio from the National Flood Insurance Program. The special report was quite impressive, especially the Rothwell fiscal impact section, which effectively dispelled doubts on SAR concerning losses on city services, and which was a remarkable product for the short period of preparation.

It should be noted that, throughout the weeks from the placement to the removal of the no-go position by the City Council, the SAR partners meet frequently to discuss their position. Many were quite pessimistic about the outcome and seriously considered selling the property at a substantial profit for one of several attractive offers, to the "butchers" so called. HUD's interest in SAR had made the site very marketable, and there were a couple of close votes on SAR policy among the partners.

The meeting of November 29, 1971, was not a regularly scheduled City Council session, but rather could be considered a public hearing on SAR. In attendance was Director Nicoson of ONCD in HUD, several other HUD officials, City Council members, County Commissioners, other agency board members and staff, city staff, private civic and environmental group representatives, and a large SAR developer contingent.

The meeting was somewhat anticlimatic and consisted of a statement by, and a long series of questions directed at, Nicoson and his HUD staff. The answers centered around assurances that nothing bad would happen to central city San Antonio if SAR should be approved, and contained positive innuendoes regarding a new town in-town. The major point of contention raised at the meeting was with respect to the divergent fiscal impact results presented by CMH and the Planning Department. City Council remanded the issue to the contending parties for reconciliation.

By early December the SAR issue was publicly almost dormant, with the complete cessation of media coverage, but the battles raged on in private. The pressures were maintained on outspoken opponents, especially City Council members. CMH invited the councilmen to a weekend hunting trip outside the city. All but Haberman and Dr. Robert L.M. Hilliard went along to what could only have promised to be a hard-sell weekend. At least one councilman reversed his position during this time, and others felt they had to make a decision soon just to relieve the constant pressure. Meanwhile, the environmentalist opposition was also lobbying to whatever extent they could. Their advantage was the collaboration of professional staff within the city and other agencies such as SARA, EUWD, and AACOG. In mid-December the board of SARA passed a resolution in opposition to SAR, and shortly the EUWD board followed similarly, opposing "any governmentally sponsored project encouraging urban development over the recharge zone of the Edwards Underground Reservoir," both expressing concerns for the aquifer. The San Antonio Independent School District also went on record as opposing SAR, because of the belief that it would draw funds, tax base, and students away from the central city. However, at the AACOG GARC meeting of December 14, 1971, a resolution moved by Garza was passed which exhorted the City Council to remove its no-go position of October 21, in order to allow time for the developers and city staff to reconcile their differences and for developers to prepare legal assurances for the city regarding the project. (The resolution further called for environmental studies to be directed by an impartial study group, prior to formal approval by HUD. This idea was later enacted by HUD.)

The next day, in a stormy Executive Committee session, Bexar County Commissioner Albert A. Pena moved that AACOG reconsider its May approval of SAR. The motion was defeated, 9-8, with the vote of Ochse who was reputed to be associated with the venture. The events of the two days at AACOG represented a genuine coup for the SAR developers, carried out by a powerful legion of proponents, led by Garza and Ochse. The vote was the first tangible evidence of a turn in the tide, since efforts had been made at both the November and December GARC meetings to reopen the SAR review that had been closed as favorable in May. Although the official AACOG position never changed after that, SAR was just as vulnerable there as elsewhere until the December GARC vote.

Two days later there was a replay at a regular meeting of the City Council. A similar motion was made by Garza, and was passed 6-3, thus removing the no-go position. In favor were Becker, Garza, Haberman, Ed H. Hill, Leo Mendoza, and Pleas Naylor; opposing were Mayor Gatti, Hilliard, and Felix B. Trevino. Spokesmen for several environmental groups again stated their positions, but to no avail. Although the resolution passed removed the no-go position in order to provide time for developer and city staff to reconcile fiscal impact assumptions and to prepare legal assurances for the city, it was generally understood that the motion was in effect reversing the previous negative stance of the city toward SAR, and adopting a neutral, wait-and-see, if not outright favorable posture toward the development of SAR. Opponents and proponents alike widely believed that the city retired for Christmas having approved SAR.

## Contract and Commitment

With the removal of the no-go by the City Council, the question of SAR's existence faded, and specific issues of controls were taken up. The developers and the city staff were still cooperating to reconcile impact analyses, but the emphasis was on a legal document which the developers had suggested to embody the assurances sought by the city. The environmentalist groups, sensing defeat, began consideration of legal action as a last resort to block the impending HUD loan guarantee commitment, as they had accomplished with the construction of the North Expressway.

The cooperation on costs and fiscal impact was something of a myth, since both developers and city staff knew that the conflict had been resolved, that Council was relieved to be free of the pressures of decision, and that the only mode of compromise remaining was the legal assurance document. The most pragmatic of the opponents realized that this document was their last hope, and therefore that it should be written as well as possible. The document, called a contract, was prepared for the City Council meeting of February 3, 1972. The primary clauses included can be summarized as follows:

1. that the SAR sewage lines be constructed for maximum protection and be connected to the regional system, and that water quality studies be conducted prior to development;
2. that the city furnish sewer service to SAR
3. that the developers assist in planning for a new town in-town
4. that the city provide water, gas, and electrical service for SAR
5. that the city retain an option on annexation of SAR, and
6. that the city have the right to block federal grants to SAR considered competitive with other city programs. [6]

Despite an opinion from the City Attorney that this contract was not enforceable, because one City Council could not bind future Councils, the contract was passed on February 3 by the same 6-3 lineup. On February 10 the Council passed a resolution favoring the development of SAR and the City's annexation thereof. With a few modifications, the contract was approved again on February 17, by the same vote, with the same caveat from the City Attorney.

Meanwhile, HUD had proceeded with the publication, on January 20, 1972, of the Final Environmental Impact Statement for SAR. This time the City of San Antonio was on the mailing list. It was a beefed-up version of the Draft EIS of the previous September, but with the myriad comments received since then rebutted point-by-point in an appendix. HUD hoped that the lengthy rebuttal would be adequate to complete the required compliance with the NEPA of 1969. The reaction of the environmental groups was a second round of outrage at noncompliance, but the groups had few allies by this time.

In February, prior to the end of the mandated 30-day circulation period for the Final EIS, the CDC in HUD met formally to hear the SAR application for loan guarantee. The ONCD staff recommendation was favorable, given the contract with the city and the publication of the Final EIS. The Board of Directors acted affirmatively, and on February 23, 1972, HUD announced that it had made a tentative offer of commitment to guarantee $18 million in loans for SAR. The offer was conditioned by a ban on any construction until antipollution measures could be studied and implemented.[7] SAR was the first HUD Title VII commitment to be conditional in such a manner. Essentially, HUD was forcing the developers to do as AACOG had called for in the GARC resolution of December 14, 1971.

On the same day as the commitment, February 23, four local private organizations—The Sierra Club, Citizens for a Better Environment, the League of Women Voters, and the American Association of University Women—filed suit in U.S. District Court for an injunction to prevent the SAR developers from accepting the proffered loan guarantee commitment. On February 24 the plaintiffs (the four organizations) and the defendants (San Antonio Ranch, Ltd., and HUD) agreed that the developers would not accept the offer of commitment prior to the scheduled March 16 full hearing.

The plaintiffs' suit was joined unexpectedly by Bexar County the next day, February 25, on a narrow 3-2 vote of the Commissioners Court. The commissioners had in November passed a resolution opposing any and all urban development on the recharge and buffer zones of the aquifer until it could be proven not to endanger the water quality. As legal action against SAR became more and more likely, Assistant District Attorney Norris Yates was requested to evaluate the feasibility of county participation in any litigation. Yates, a Republican and former associate of SAR attorney Seagal Wheatley, returned predictably with a negative recommendation. County Judge Blair Reeves, virtually ignoring Yates' counsel, completed his turn-about from support of SAR to opposition by enthusiastically leading the majority of the Commissioners into joining the suit. Reeves claimed his earlier endorsement of SAR had been based on the increase SAR would cause on the county tax rolls, while the risk to the

aquifer ultimately changed his mind. Commissioner Pena had been
a consistent foe of SAR from the beginning, charging that it was a big
federal handout to developers. Commissioner A.J. Ploch apparently
still rankled over the UTSA site location in the northwest, and was
determined to oppose any collateral development. Of the two negative
votes, Commissioner Frank Vaughan claimed to be against SAR but
also against entering the suit, while Commissioner Tom Stolhandske
apparently was the sole supporter of SAR all along.

One last public agency, the Edwards Underground Water District,
joined the plaintiffs in the suit on March 14. In an unanimous board
action, the EUWD acted consistent with a policy statement of January
11, 1972, that EUWD would take positions and legal action in the future
on any proposals endangering the aquifer. Honts had made a last appeal
to the EUWD board just prior to their vote to intervene in the legal
action. The SARA board, on the other hand, which had in December
passed a resolution opposing SAR, voted not to join the suit. Reasons
that have been advanced for this seeming change of heart include strong
pressure on each director from the developers, especially Head, and
the close functional ties between SARA and the TWQB, which had joined
the suit on the side of the defendants on March 10 (ostensibly to protect
its statutory domain in water quality matters from local and regional
agency interlopers and from adverse judicial interpretation).

Also on March 14, 1972, U.S. District Judge Adrian A. Spears
granted a motion by SAR developers that the case be held in abeyance
pending their compliance with the provisions of a nine-point proposal.
The key points involved were that

1. SAR and HUD conduct tests on the aquifer, to be monitored by a
   review board of local agencies
2. HUD update and expand the "Final EIS" of January and circulate
   it again
3. The Court retain supervision of the case and be informed of all
   action by HUD on SAR
4. SAR developers agree not to accept the offer of commitment until
   the suit be resolved[8]

According to the HUD regulations, the developers would have 120 days
in which to accept the offer of commitment. However, SAR was granted
a second 120 days, and later a third and fourth such period, by HUD,
pending the completion of the litigation.

With the abeyance order, a very frenzied period in the development of SAR came to an end. What has occurred since that time has
been less hysterical and more characterized by rational arguments,
both for legal and tactical purposes, from both proponents and opponents. SAR at this point was in its judicial review period.

The Water Quality Advisory Review Board

After the Court order, the SAR developers swung immediately into action with their scientific studies and their review board of local agencies. Dr. L.J. Turk was hired to head the team of experts in the studies of storm water runoff, ground water quality, and geology of the SAR site. Generally the studies were commissioned, designed, and initiated, and then the board was convened to review the progress and to make technical suggestions to the researchers.

The technical studies involved sampling and testing the quality of storm water runoff on the SAR site and a control urbanized area (Colonies North subdivision), investigating the renovative capability of SAR site soils (Radian Corporation), geological mapping of the SAR site, and development of a system for long-term monitoring of water quality (Dr. W.H. Espey). In addition, the technicians and other SAR staff would be devising workable solutions to many of the frequently mentioned hazards implicit in the SAR development over the aquifer recharge zone, such as sanitary sewage collection and treatment, transportation and storage of dangerous liquids, solid waste collection and disposal, storm water controls, and inspection and enforcement mechanisms.

The first SAR Water Quality Advisory Review Board (WQARB) meeting was held April 24, 1972. The Board composition was determined by the SAR developers who issued the invitations: only public agencies were represented. Four federal agencies were included: Soil Conservation Service, Environmental Protection Agency, U.S. Geological Survey, and the Bureau of Outdoor Recreation. Six state agencies were invited, including TWQB, Division of Planning Coordination, Department of Health, Parks and Wildlife Department, Bureau of Economic Geology, and the Texas Water Development Board. Bexar County, AACOG, EUWD, and SARA were also represented, along with several components of the City of San Antonio (CWB, Public Works, Parks and Recreation, and Metropolitan Health District). The ONCD in HUD also sent an "observer" to each meeting. Of this group, only Bexar County, EUWD, and SARA were publicly opposed to the development of SAR. Noticeably absent from the list of invitations were the San Antonio Planning Department and the City Manager's Office.

The WQARB was a carefully orchestrated exercise in public relations, under the cover of scientific enlightenment. Hugh Yantis of TWQB was preselected to chair the Board; no public official in the state had done more already for the development of SAR. With

Honts setting the agenda, Turk presenting the technical materials for review, and Yantis adroitly fielding questions from the Board participants, the WQARB sessions were masterpieces in controlled citizen participation technique, in fulfillment of Court and HUD demands.

Further WQARB meetings were held on May 11, June 8, and June 23. Only at the final session were any representatives of private organizations with environmental concerns asked to attend. At that time a few such representatives made the expected disparaging remarks regarding the WQARB, but the atmosphere had been already sterilized by careful concentration on technological solutions, and consequently the attacks fell on deaf ears. Even the public agency delegations who opposed SAR were surprisingly muted during the meetings, asking only perfunctory technical questions from time to time.

At the final session no attempt was made to pass any resolution approving the already completed or as yet incomplete studies. Yantis, however, announced that he would take the studies and their outputs to his TWQB meeting the next week for approval. Several participants vehemently objected, since such endorsement would implicitly legitimatize the tentative findings of the developer's consultants, under the auspices of the WQARB. But there was little that such objections could accomplish.

The TWQB did indeed formally adopt the results of the studies, in an order stating to HUD that the SAR plans formulated under the eye of a cross section of state, local, and regional agencies would protect the aquifer. Lou Rosenberg, by then an attorney representing several opposition environmental groups, and Fred Pfeiffer of SARA protested the TWQB action vigorously as conferring legitimacy on studies conducted not impartially but by the SAR developers. Rosenberg squared off against TWQB Chairman Gordon Fulcher on the subject of private versus public interests, but in the end the preordained TWQB action prevailed.

Concurrent with the SAR Water Quality Advisory Review Board were manifestations of a couple of new directions being plotted by environmentalists both public and private. The four organizations involved in the SAR suit as plaintiffs sponsored a colloquium concerning "Positive Options for San Antonio's Future Water Quality," held May 1, 1972, at the Gunter Hotel. The environmentalist groups, snubbed by Honts in the invitations for the WQARB, had decided to host a water quality session of their own. They had also resolved to focus their attack on positive proposals, rather than continually being forced to the negative side, as in the SAR controversy. The Gunter meeting, therefore, represented something of a counteroffensive for the environmentally concerned citizens, with an emphasis on preserving the aquifer. Honts considered the meeting enough of an attack on SAR to dispatch two of his important local lieutenants, B. J. (Red) McCombs and Jose (Pepe) Lucero, to dispute various points and to heckle the proceedings. Speakers included several persons active in the SAR opposition, including Lou Rosenberg and Robert Sohn, the new CBE president. But the thrust of the meeting was in the direction of potential legal controls on land use in the aquifer area in Bexar County and possible outright purchase of the recharge zone in the county. The latter stirred most of the excitement, but the cost, estimated at $70 million, was thought excessive for serious consideration.

However, late in May, Representative Henry B. Gonzalez spoke out in favor of purchase of the recharge zone as an alternative to surface water development costs. Gonzalez, unusually quiet throughout the SAR conflict, did not refer to SAR and was not very specific on the purchase plan, but condemned the failure of public agencies to regulate development on the recharge zone. Gonzalez' speech sparked several efforts to investigate feasibility of such purchase action, but nothing resulted from them at the time.


New Town in-Town


Suddenly in June word leaked to the public about a proposed new town in-town for San Antonio, being planned and financed through Christian, Miller, and Honts, the prime members of the SAR development team. The new town (known simply as San Antonio New Town) was to be located on 558 acres immediately to the north of the Central Business District, and with the San Antonio River as its spine. Any plans prepared would be based on private entrepreneurship in conjuntion with urban renewal authority for land acquisition. It was also understood that the new town would be developed as a HUD Title VII new community similar to SAR.

Several people in San Antonio had known of the new town proposal for several weeks prior to disclosure. The primary local backers, especially Red McCombs and William Ochse, had made several contacts for potential investors. In addition, San Antonio Development Agency (SADA, formerly Urban Renewal Agency) director Winston Martin and, much later, Mayor Gatti had also been informed. But Honts and his local development group had also approached Charles Kilpatrick and Frank Bennack, publishers, respectively, of the two major newspapers, the Express-News and the Light, demanding a news blackout until some appropriate future time for full announcement. The argument for this demand was that the speculation and interference which might be touched off, as well as any remaining fallout from the SAR controversy, could be severely damaging to the young and vulnerable new town project; to willfully damage the new town would be to deal a blow to downtown development, which every civic-minded citizen must be for. Bennack agreed easily, but Kilpatrick consented reluctantly to this abridgement of freedom of the press (as he had had to do during the heat of the SAR conflict), until public officials divulged the story. Express-News reporter Deborah Weser eventually discovered the new town and pursued the scoop, only to have Honts issue a press release on the new town on the eve of publication, after learning of her story.

SANT had originally been conceived by CMH as the logical means of neutralizing much of the opposition to SAR. HUD Assistant Secretary Jackson had even suggested to CMH during the fall of 1971 that such a course of action be investigated. At much the same time HUD had become enthusiastic about the concept of paired new communities— a suburban satellite town linked in facilities, transportation, and spirit with a new town in-town. In addition, the HUD New Communities Program was vulnerable to increasing charges of catering to suburban developers exclusively, since only one new town in-town, and none of the free-standing or add-on types, had as yet been approved. Consequently HUD was quite encouraging to Honts when he started the preliminary planning and application procedure for a new town in-town for San Antonio.

Thus, with HUD looking favorably at the new town concept, with a perceived need to offset SAR as a hot and negative issue, and with the potential for a genuinely good, lucrative development project, Honts felt he needed only to sell the new town in-town locally in San Antonio. He had ultimately succeeded in selling SAR, but at an enormous cost in resources and image. But the new town in-town was different. Most of the important public officials who had balked at SAR had done so because of the potential competition for funds with the inner city—downtown was higher on their list of priorities. To present these officials all of a sudden with the new town in-town that they had used to symbolize their priorities would be a major coup for Honts, leaving no option but support.

Indeed, when the news of SANT became public, there was consternation and surprise, but hardly a negative word. There were warnings from key public officials like Mayor Gatti to go slowly and examine every detail, but the general reaction could only be positive. Honts' early strategy was a whirlwind round of local agency endorsements for the project, coupled with a judicious manipulation of the strong Republican political priorities for Texas in the 1972 election, to win approval for SANT from HUD by November. Accordingly, he set out to approach each relevant public body and individual in the local area, to wave before them their statements during the SAR controversy about a new town in-town, and then politely to demand an endorsement of the SANT concept and plans. Further required approvals, such as A-95 review, would have to be obtained later.

During the months subsequent to June he gained in regular succession the backing of SADA, the Planning Commission, the City Council, both newspapers, AACOG, and the River Corridor Committee. This last was a multiagency creation to supervise a HUD-funded study of the San Antonio River and Urban Corridor, a 7 1/2-mile stretch of the river with the downtown at its center. SANT was to be located entirely within the study area. The agencies involved were the city, the county, SADA, AACOG, SARA, and the San Antonio Independent School District. Their approval of SANT was both essential and significant.

Also of importance for HUD approval was the CMH effort to broaden the base of involvement in SANT over that of SAR. One of the key associates was Pepe Lucero, a consultant formerly connected with antipoverty agencies in San Antonio. Honts was making a pitch to minority group investors to join the new town in-town in order to lessen the SAR group's financial commitment, as well as for public relations purposes—to appear more balanced locally and better to meet HUD's criteria on participation.

In the early stages of SANT debate, the major point of contention again was one of competition for federal funds. Many professionals and some public officials expressed concern that, if approved by HUD, the new town in-town—which would require an urban renewal Neighborhood Development Program (NDP) as an implementation vehicle—would preclude funds for a proposed ten-block downtown mall development and for a small NDP on the predominantly black East Side. But these arguments, although potentially quite important, did not gain any supporters among key public officials. It would have been political suicide to have opposed SANT at that point after the bitter SAR experience.

The SANT Pre-Application was submitted to ONCD in HUD in August 1972. Although some revisions were necessary, the go-ahead was given almost immediately to CMH to proceed with the Final Application. The way for passage through HUD was apparently already well smoothed, or else SANT would have had to wait its turn on a long list of Pre-Applications for review by ONCD. The preparation of Final Application materials ran somewhat behind the tight schedule that had been set, and individual items were being submitted frantically to ONCD throughout October 1972, in order to receive some tentative favorable feedback prior to election day in November, since the high priority of the project in HUD was related to the exigencies of the political campaign. (George Christian of CMH had become communications director for John Connally's Democrats-for-Nixon group during the campaign, and was included, along with Hayden Head, at the elegant political barbecues Connally gave for Nixon at his ranch. Nixon's reelection staff made no secret of their belief that Texas was a "must" state for Nixon to carry in order to win the election.) The day before the elections, Senator John Tower announced at City Hall that a special task force in HUD had ruled favorably on SANT, calling it "unique," and had assigned it the "highest priority" for final approval. This unprecedented action was a consolation prize for not winning the race to election day with the SANT application.

Throughout the debate over SANT, the activities of Honts and his associates were characterized by their accustomed secrecy, broken only for important presentations. After the initial public announcement of SANT in June, Honts had promised maximum cooperation, coordination, input, and review for all public agencies involved. But despite a brief flurry of meetings at the beginning, the San Antonio Planning Department, SADA, and AACOG, among others on the River Corridor Committee (all of which felt they were entitled to close cooperation in all planning activities), were effectively excluded from all but superficial liaison. None had even been apprised of the status of the Final Application at the time of the Tower announcement.

After Tower's election-eve appearance, Honts and SANT disappeared again, but surfaced quickly in January 1973, after President Nixon proclaimed a freeze on funds for many urban programs which "weren't working," including HUD's NDP, subsidized housing, and other categorical grant funds important to new communities, to many of which SANT was inextricably tied. Those programs were to be frozen after June 30, and Honts once again began to scramble. Ironically, HUD appeared to have lost interest in SANT (now that the election was over and new faces were taking over the top positions) as a spokesman labeled its chances "unlikely." The formal reviews and approvals by AACOG (the A-95 process) and the City Council (for renewal activities) were moved up earlier than originally planned. In February and March, AACOG's GARC and Executive Committee passed favorable review on SANT, the River Corridor Committee formally endorsed it, and the City Council issued another tentative approval. In addition, two bills were introduced into the Texas Legislature to alter the state urban renewal law to enable the city and SANT to cooperate. And late in March HUD released the draft Environmental Impact Statement for SANT, which, although once again prepared by the developer team, was thorough and fair (although incomplete in some social aspects) and caused little stir.

At the end of March, big trouble materialized for SANT—U.S. Representative Henry B. Gonzalez launched an attack on the proposed legislative changes in the urban renewal laws which he himself had helped frame back in the 1950s. Gonzalez, long silent during the SAR controversy, had erupted some weeks earlier against the SAR proposal to create a municipal utility district as a financing and governing device. Gonzalez' intense lobbying of selected legislators over the next couple of months certainly had a major role in killing the SANT legislation. The bills themselves, which would have enabled SADA to work with a single preselected redeveloper (SANT), and would have permitted subsidies in the form of long-term real property tax abatement, were objected to by Gonzalez on the grounds of creating "private land monopolies" in downtown areas to which public subsidies would be fed. By May his charges had escalated into his famed hyperbole, as he claimed the city would "surrender all public powers and large amounts of public money to a monopoly." By this time also, Gonzalez produced a SANT investor prospectus for his House Government Operations subcommittee which stated that SANT investors could obtain an after-tax return of as much as 100 percent through the public assistance, and was threatening a subcommittee investigation of both SANT and SAR "questionable deals"—"I want to pick up the rocks and see what's crawling around . . . there is a lot of jiggery pokery going on."[9]

Combined, the effect of Gonzalez on both the legislature and the City Council was substantial. The renewal bills had been introduced to the legislature on the consent calendar—a docket for local items only—which generally passes automatically. They passed the House without a blink, behind strong inside lobbying from CMH, but stumbled in the Senate when Gonzalez persuaded a few senators to "tag" the bills, virtual death for consent items, especially at the end of a session. Thus by the end of May the needed legislation was doomed.

Meanwhile in San Antonio the new town in-town issue had stimulated a great deal of lively debate. The City Council had twice given its general acquiescence to the project, but without the detailed review and the public hearings that it was felt to warrant. In April an almost totally new council was seated in the biennial elections. SANT was a minor issue in those elections, appearing only in comic relief for a last-minute verbal joust between outgoing Mayor Gatti and his aspiring successor Charles Becker. The latter claimed to have been offered a piece of SANT investment by Bob Honts, and that Gatti received such an offer too, but said both had rejected the proposed investment as improper. Gatti denied the matter altogether and called Becker "a pathological liar." In any event, the new council included only three holdovers from the previous one, and Becker was elected mayor.

While the last-minute lobbying was taking place in the Legislature on the renewal bills for SANT, the new City Council was considering the project in great detail. A growing number of critics of the new town was emerging, especially businessmen left out of the project or adversely affected by its location. Continued probing and staff review uncovered some features of the plans and proposals that incited further opposition. One was the admission by Honts that the developers would be reselling at a large profit some publicly subsidized land to which no "development" would actually be done (except applying deed restrictions). Another was the matter of excessive profits, which Honts claimed would be necessary for some parcels in order to offset losses on others, such as the required low-income housing. A third point for opposition was the inclusion for housing reuse of a 10-acre parcel adjacent to a parochial high school which school officials had designated for playing-fields expansion. The opposition began to snowball as only opposition can: the new council was not ready for positive action itself, only for blocking what could be a damaging proposal from others. Mayor Becker opened up with his favorite theme: "Everybody complains about the high taxes, yet they expect a federal grant to fall into their laps for everything. Now it's time for people in private enterprise to do their thing. This country wasn't built on federal programs."[10] He made a counterproposal that the new town be undertaken entirely with local private corporate funding. To underscore his rationale, he challenged black councilman Rev. Claude W. Black, who supported the federal role as an equalizer: "I'll bet the best suit of clothes in town that we'll take the competitive sector and you take the public sector and we'll back 'em off the face of the earth."[11]

Nevertheless, when it came to voting on SANT, on May 17, 1973, Becker joined the majority for a 7-2 endorsement of the new town in-town, which reserved, however, the designation of the actual redevelopment entity to execute the project, thus finally begging the public versus private issue. The approval was rendered moot by the Legislature's withholding of the renewal law changes necessary to the SANT project. In mid-June Honts revealed that HUD had placed SANT on its "inactive" list of new community applicants, at the request of the SANT development team. With that, the new town in-town quietly passed from the scene.

A MUD For SAR

While the whole new town in-town debate was occurring over the course of a year, a new unexpected catalyst ignited the SAR fireworks again. In February 1973, almost a year after the final City Council vote, the contract, and the filing of the suit, news leaked out of a proposal by the SAR developers for the creation of a municipal utility district (MUD) on the SAR site. These districts were a creation of the 1971 legislature to promote the efficient implacement of water and sewer systems in new developments. They have proliferated ever since, especially in fast-growing urban areas. MUDs are actually quasi-governmental entities, with bond issuance and taxation powers, and a not very limited range of municipal facilities on which to spend the bond funds. A board of directors, composed of district landowners, is required to oversee floating of bonds, taxes for repayment, and the disbursement of funds thus raised. The potential benefits to developers, as well as potential abuses, are numerous, but center around the ability to obtain large-scale funding for capital costs of development infrastructure, which is repaid by residents after the developer has withdrawn. All of the powers for such actions rest with one man or one company (through the appointed board, subsequently elected by landowners—that is, the developer, at first). [12]

In the SAR case, the developers decided that a MUD was needed after the announced cutoff of many federal categorical grant funds, to be effective July 1, 1973. Such grants had been a critical component in the delicate feasibility equation of the SAR project. The MUD concept was an acceptable substitute for financing $28 million in development infrastructure, and also solved some knotty problems concerning a mode of governance for SAR prior to annexation by the City of San Antonio. Since the SAR team owned all of the 3,166 acres of the total site (early development staging areas) proposed for the MUD, no problems were likely to be encountered in gathering signatures on a petition to the Texas Water Rights Commission (TWRC) for official approval of the MUD. It was deemed advisable, however, to seek the endorsement of the San Antonio City Council prior to filing a request with the TWRC. At that point, the proposal became public and a new outcry began.

Honts attempted to sneak the MUD proposal onto the City Council agenda (with top staff and council acquiescence) without stirring the deep passions regarding SAR that lay barely submerged around the city. Someone in the City Manager's Office leaked out news of the proposal two days before the council meeting. The reaction was swift and intense, as Bexar County Judge Reeves and the Express both loudly demanded a delay for further study of the proposal. The council agreed to a week's postponement.

During that week, however, Representative Henry B. Gonzalez jumped into the fray. Up to this point Gonzalez had chosen to remain neutral and silent in the SAR political mess, an uncharacteristic posture for one so attentive to local affairs. In the matter of the MUD, though, Gonzalez acted with a strongly worded message to the City Council urging defeat of the proposal. The council ignored him and the other opposition and endorsed the MUD, 7-1 (only Alvin Padilla dissenting). Gonzalez condemned the action by the "lame duck" council for moving with "unprecedented haste" to approve "an unprecedented leap into tax liabilities that will be imposed on generations yet to be born," and then sent a letter to Secretary James T. Lynn of HUD objecting to the MUD and HUD's tacit support of it. The HUD reply of a few weeks later called the issue "complex" and requiring further study.

In early March 1973 the SAR developers officially filed an application with the TWRC for the establishment of Municipal Utility District No. 1 on the SAR property. At about the same time the plaintiffs in the suit against SAR claimed to the presiding judge that the City Council action on the MUD violated the injunction order granted the previous year pending trial. Upon the recommendation of the judge, the SAR development team later voluntarily withdrew the TWRC application until the end of the trial.

As it eventually turned out, the TWRC finally opened a hearing on the MUD in early May, continued it to late May, then June, then July, then October, and finally approved the application on December 10, 1973, by a 2-to-1 vote, with a proposed board of directors and certain conditions attached. Under Gonzalez' continual prodding, the state legislature had in May amended the MUD enabling statute, including among many changes a bonded indebtedness limit, an annual audit by the TWRC, notification to the host county and neighboring cities, and requirements for public notice of elections, meetings, tax rates, and office locations.[13] These amendments remedied some of the abuses that Gonzalez and others had been carping about. The directors of the SAR MUD, temporary until elections could be held, were developer associates, three from San Antonio, one from Corpus Christi, and one from White Settlement (near Fort Worth), all of whom had bought small tracts of SAR for $10 each to become landowners in the MUD. The conditions attached to the MUD by the TWRC excluded additional infrastructure requirements imposed on SAR by HUD or the TWQB from funding by MUD bonds and prohibited use of such funds for preparation for utility lines on adjacent property. Together, the legislature's amendments and the TWRC conditions greatly alleviated the potential for abuse of the MUD by the developers and enhanced the credibility of the SAR situation.

The MUD potential was finally actuated in late October 1974, after the completion of SAR litigation, with the election of a board of directors and the authorization of the issuance of $26,896,000 in bonds by the six resident electors in the district.

## Pretrial Maneuvering

Well over a year elapsed between the filing of the suit against SAR and the trial to decide the case. First, the four plaintiff organizations had been joined in the suit by the EUWD and Bexar County, then the named defendants—SAR and HUD—were joined by the TWQB, which claimed the right to protect its authority and jurisdiction. Shortly thereafter the SAR developers successfully petitioned Judge Spears to hold the case in abeyance pending the outcome of the studies undertaken for the WQARB. The abeyance order effectively became an injunction on further activity on SAR until the trial, since the results of the studies were not to be reviewed until then.

On August 24, 1972, following the completion of the WQARB meetings, an Addendum to the Final Environmental Impact Statement on SAR was released by HUD, again with a request for comments from public agencies, but also including certain private organizations as well. The Addendum was much better written than its predecessors —almost, as one observer remarked, with the precision of a legal document prepared by attorneys. The Addendum, as with the preceding statements, was written for HUD by the SAR developer staff and consultants, in close to routine violation of the letter and spirit of the NEPA of 1969.

In terms of content, the Addendum was far more complete than the other statements in its treatment of each environmental hazard posed by SAR, the regional planning documents pertaining to natural resources, and the alternatives to the proposed action. The Addendum accepted the findings of the developer studies conducted under the nominal auspices of the WQARB. In addition, HUD had contracted with another geological consultant, Henry V. Beck of Kansas State University, who had nothing but praise for the developer technical studies and concurred wholeheartedly in the findings. Once again, comments poured in from the 38 agencies and groups on the official list of distribution, some concerning the same and further environmental aspects of SAR, others with growth patterns, funding conflicts, and legal controls. The Community and Environmental Standards Office (CESO) and the Environmental Clearance Section of the General Counsel's Office in HUD evaluated the comments for possible inclusion in a project agreement or an appendix to the Addendum. On September 25, 1972, just over 30 days from the issuance of the Addendum, the CDC declared all conditions met and authorized the execution of a project agreement with SAR.

In October 1972 the SAR attorneys requested a hearing on the plaintiffs' suit in U.S. District Court. They demanded that Bexar County withdraw from the suit, due to a legal requirement for a county to be represented solely by its District Attorney, not by a private attorney, as the plaintiffs had in Phillip D. Hardberger. The Bexar County District Attorney, Ted Butler, was publicly opposed (along with his assistant Yates) to the participation of the county in the suit, and was unlikely to take an active role in its behalf. The request was taken under advisement and was rendered moot by the assignment of an assistant district attorney to the case. The SAR attorneys also demanded that the financial sources of the Aquifer Defense Fund of the plaintiff groups be made public, claiming they had violated a rule against "solicitation of business by lawyers" in raising funds. This demand was rejected.

Funds for the plaintiffs' suit were becoming of critical importance by this time, however. The four original plaintiff groups had expended much of their resources in combatting the North Expressway, and were not in strong financial position for a long court battle. Funds were adequate to launch the suit, with some donation of time by Hardberger, and were relieved by the entrance of the EUWD and Bexar County, each contributing several thousand dollars. The plaintiffs realized that to pursue the case properly would take a long time, and would necessitate undertaking professional studies of the aquifer to counteract the SAR developer-commissioned studies. Consequently, the groups were soliciting funds wherever they could for "aquifer protection," a thinly disguised cover for SAR prosecution. The chief support they discovered was in the local breweries. These breweries, Lone Star and Pearl, were genuinely concerned about the quality of untreated water in the aquifer, which was responsible, more than any other factor, for the distinctive taste of their beer products. They wished to assist the environmental groups in their efforts to keep urban development from the recharge zone where it could pollute the aquifer water. But they were also fearful of the antagonism, reprisals, and bad publicity they could expect if their aid became known to some SAR supporters, such as Councilman Becker, the owner of Handy Andy food stores—largest single buyer of the local beers. As a result, the breweries were at first equivocal in their position, but then agreed to contribute to the Aquifer Defense Fund. Later, the environmental groups hosted a moderately successful AquiFair, as part of Aquifer Week, which raised some more funds, mostly in small donations.

Throughout the fall of 1972 the funds problems were causing serious tensions within the plaintiff coalition. It became known that Hardberger wanted out of the suit, because of what some sources described as financial stress from receiving less in fees from the groups than he had expected, and/or what others claimed was disillusionment over perceived emotionalism rather than professionalism on the part of the environmental groups involved. In addition, conflict between the Bexar County Commissioners and the District Attorney, as well as disagreements among the commissioners themselves, did not bode well for continued strong county participation in the suit. Even the EUWD, being pressed hard by the TWQB, might not be able to continue as a viable ally. Furthermore, SAR was declining as a visible public issue around which the environmental organizations could catalyze their memberships for a strong continuing mandate in the suit. Doubts increased that the existing plaintiff coalition could not persevere beyond the first decision of the court.

At a pretrial hearing at the end of December 1972, Judge Spears scheduled the trial itself to begin in late January. Soon thereafter it was postponed until March, and finally to April 30, 1973, at the request of Bexar County, whose assistant district attorney on the case suddenly died and necessitated a new assignment and further preparation. At another pretrial hearing in March, Judge Spears denied a motion from the SAR defendants for a summary judgment in the case, to eliminate the need for a full trial, based on the issuance of the addendum to the Final EIS. He set the April 30 trial date and declared the issue to be decided at the trial to be

> whether the decision of [former HUD Secretary George Romney] was arbitrary, capricious, or an abuse of discretion, or other wise not in accordance with law. Implicit in this is the question "whether the Environmental Impact Statement complies with the requirements of NEPA and the Federal Guidelines and with the Housing and Urban Development Act of 1970."[14]

Spears stated that he intended to make a "substantial inquiry" based upon a "thorough, probing, in-depth review" of the Secretary's decision at the trial. The opposing attorneys indicated at this pretrial hearing that there could be as many as 54 witnesses testifying at the trial for both sides.


SAR on Trial


The trial finally opened on April 30, 1973, in U.S. District Court in San Antonio. It lasted for nine days of testimony, chiefly concerning water quality and urban growth patterns. The general strategy of the plaintiffs was to convince the judge that SAR represented a clear danger to the water supply which was deliberately overlooked by HUD in its decision to approve SAR and in its EIS documents, and that SAR's location was de facto evidence that the urban growth and equal opportunity goals underlying the New Communities Program had not been followed in the decision. The tactics of the defense attorneys would be to discredit the plaintiff witnesses, since the burden of proof was on them, and to demonstrate that perfectly legal procedures had been adhered to in the HUD review and approval of SAR and that inordinately strong measures had been imposed to avert pollution of the aquifer.

The defense was based on maintaining as narrow a case as possible, and on avoiding any justification of SAR itself with all its weaknesses. The plaintiffs' legal team was headed by Hardberger, the attorney hired by the private organizations in the suit, who was supported by the new assistant district attorney representing Bexar County on the case, Keith W. Burris, and the counsel for the EUWD. The defense attorneys included Seagal Wheatley, former U.S. District Attorney and Bexar County Republican chairman, as well as counsel from HUD and the TWQB.

The opening few days of the trial were taken up with tedious technical recitations by scientists and engineers called by the plaintiffs. The cast of experts comprised: Dr. Sergio Garza, an hydrologist with the U.S. Geological Survey; Ken Cave, a SARA water quality engineer; Dr. Calvin H. Ward, an environmental sciences professor at Rice University; and Dr. Zane Spiegel, an hydrologist from Santa Fe, New Mexico. For three days these witnesses lectured theoretically, conducted high school type experiments, and presented lessons from similar cases elsewhere. All concluded that SAR posed a significant threat to water quality in the Edwards Aquifer.

The environmental issues discussed during this phase of the trial generally concerned potential problems SAR could cause the recharge zone of the aquifer—stemming from storm runoff from urbanized surfaces, disposal of sanitary sewage from the new community, and handling of dangerous substances such as gasoline in underground storage tanks, as well as technical questions such as what quantity of pollutants entering the aquifer would constitute intolerable pollution of San Antonio's water and how best to measure the pollution. The contentions of the plaintiff experts could be summarized as (1) that pollutants entering the aquifer at SAR would probably contaminate the areas of the wells from which San Antonio draws its water; (2) that all sewer lines leak to some degree; (3) that the approved leakage rate for SAR could total millions of gallons a day overall; (4) that there are so many fractures in the limestone on the recharge zone that pollution could not help but reach the aquifer; (5) that the water quality studies conducted by the SAR developers were inadequate to ensure protection of the aquifer; and (6) that the technological measures planned for SAR to prevent pollution were untried and unproven.

In cross-examination, every expert witness was impugned in some manner regarding his professional integrity or familiarity with the SAR data, as well as the logic of his conclusions. Judge Spears listened intently, asking numerous probing questions, but nevertheless informed the attorneys that at least 60 percent of this early testimony could have been omitted.

With the next witness for the plaintiffs, San Antonio Planning Director Davis, the debate shifted to urban growth concerns. Davis, who had taken a strong stance against SAR in instigating the general controversy in late 1971, was at the time of the trial under heavy attack himself from many sides. Local developers had managed to remove the zoning and subdivision office from his control, new Mayor Becker had vowed during the City Council campaign to remove Davis as planning director (an "obstructionist," said Becker), even though a mayor could not legally fire city staff, and Davis had been isolated by the city manager in City Hall circles and in effect demoted in position. Davis held on until July 1973, at which time he resigned to assume a position in a private firm. The inflexible position Davis had maintained throughout on SAR typified the reasons that developers, and later city staff, considered his ouster from the Planning Department a necessity.

Davis' testimony focused on the planners' conclusion that balanced growth in the San Antonio area meant reversing the strong recent trends to the north. SAR to the northwest represented the largest single development unit in continuing this trend and making further growth inevitable, thus directly contradicting stated aims of the New Communities Program. Balanced growth was interpreted as meaning efficient utilization and expansion of urban services and utilities. Future growth to the south, moreover, would avert further additional costs that would be incurred by developing on the recharge zone, due to high costs of blasting the limestone subsurface and of creating alternate sources of water for the region. In addition, Davis cited evidence to support the plaintiffs' contention that superior alternative sites for new communities existed in Bexar County and were not considered by HUD, in violation of NEPA.

Bexar County Judge Blair Reeves took the stand as the final witness for the plaintiffs. In a dramatic moment in the trial, Reeves confessed that his early endorsement of SAR, out of which a great deal of mileage had been made by the SAR developers, had been a mistake and that he should not have done it. He proceeded to describe how his old friend John Peace, then chairman of the University of Texas Board of Regents, had introduced Hayden Head to him with praise for the proposed SAR development which could do much for the County. Reeves then agreed to write his favorable letter.

During the course of all this testimony by the plaintiff witnesses, presiding Judge Spears occasionally interrupted, speaking as a "concerned citizen and taxpayer," to lament the seemingly hopeless plight of the aquifer and its recharge zone.

> The national, state, county and city governments should
> do something about it—not just talk about it. . . . Why
> isn't someone doing something other than just study, plan
> and propose? Nothing is not an alternative to something.

. . . Ideally, all that [aquifer] area should be fenced off, trees, parks, bridle paths—not for horses, maybe. There's going to be more and more pollution because that's the way things have been going. At what point in time are we going to find where the whole area will be polluted?[15]

But in partial answer he also injected a note of realism tied to the case at hand: "The entire area is going to be developed; so the thing that it seems to me is that as far as the people are concerned they have to do the best they can with the property that is being developed."[16] Thus Judge Spears listened to the plaintiffs' arguments, was affected by them personally—outraged even by the obvious inconsistencies between problem and resolution—but realized at the same time that he was trying a specific case on the narrow grounds of federal statutory law.

On the fifth day of the SAR trial, plaintiff attorney Hardberger rested his case, and the defense began. The first witness called was Dr. Turk, the UT-Austin geologist who had conducted the majority of the SAR developer environmental studies. Turk testified mainly that the monitoring wells would detect any pollution in time for remedial action, and that the chances of error were miniscule. But he conceded under cross-examination the possibility of leakage into the aquifer of liquids from sewer pipes and underground storage tanks. Turk argued, however, that any pollutants entering the aquifer at SAR would be carried by the underground flows away from San Antonio water wells and toward New Braunfels and San Marcos to the northeast. This point contradicted Spiegel's testimony, but did not impress Judge Spears, who voiced concern about pollution of the entire area, not only San Antonio.

After three days on the stand, Turk was followed by his associates in the SAR water quality studies, William H. Espey, an Austin engineer, and Gus Fruh, a UT-Austin environmental health engineer. They primarily described their parts in the studies, and corroborated Turk's conclusions. Fruh also scored with the point that the City of San Antonio's standards for raw sewage leakage were less than one-fifth as stringent as those to be allowed for SAR. Finally, Henry V. Beck of Kansas State, who had been hired by HUD to review Turk's group's SAR studies, testified that the investigations had been adequate and that HUD had been justified in approving the project.

The last defense witness was HUD's representative, Anthony P. DeVito, of the Applications and Review Division in the ONCD. DeVito had played a leading role on HUD's end throughout, from the original reviews to the delicate governmental relations maneuvers to the defense of the HUD position during the litigation. On the stand, he praised SAR as a good project for all people in the San Antonio area, and took issue with Davis on whether SAR fulfilled the criteria of the New Communities Program. He concluded by defending HUD and SAR on narrow grounds—that no single new community could do everything for everybody; that because development would occur on the recharge zone in any event, the planned new community concept would best control it; and that by law HUD responds only to developer initiatives in new community location decisions, thus addressing the question of alternative sites. Finally, in answer to a query from Judge Spears, he proclaimed that HUD would enforce the terms of the development agreement with SAR, even to the point of taking over the project. DeVito was then rebutted for the plaintiffs by Catherine Powell, a Trinity University instructor, who demonstrated that SAR's location would mostly preclude access by poor and minority persons in San Antonio and offered a strategy for control of land over the aquifer recharge zone to keep it out of development.

In closing arguments at the end of the marathon ninth day of the trial, Hardberger recited the entire litany of the anti-SAR case. He asserted that SAR would not help the central city of San Antonio, would hurt the city's economic strength, would pollute and degrade the water supply, would fail to assist the poor, would unbalance urban growth, and would increase dependence on automobiles. Wheatley did not refute these points in his closing argument, instead homing in on the narrow legal issue of compliance with federal law, which after all was the subject of the litigation. Judge Spears took the case under advisement to reach a decision. Before adjourning the court, however, the judge hinted at the outcome, questioning how he could deny SAR the right to build when UTSA was being constructed in the same area. Admitting that he personally could discover little wrong in HUD's decision on SAR, he also asked rhetorically where SAR had failed to do anything required of them to protect the environment. But he concluded: "What has concerned me about this lawsuit is not just the lawsuit, but the many very overriding questions. . . . If this trial had done nothing more than to alarm the public about the water, then it has served its purpose."[17]

## Judgments and Appeals

Judge Spears delivered his decision in the SAR suit on May 21, 1973, only a few days after the end of the trial. Spears found for the defendants:

Based upon the foregoing very substantial inquiry, and recognizing that the Secretary's decision is entitled to the

presumption of regularity, and that this Court is not
empowered to substitute its judgment for that of the Secretary, the conclusion has been reached, and the finding
herein made, that the decision of the Secretary in this
cause was neither arbitrary, nor capricious, nor a clear
error of judgment, nor an abuse of discretion. On the contrary, the Court finds and concludes that the Secretary's
decision, made after full consideration of all aspects of the
problems involved, was in full compliance with the law.
Similarly, the Court finds and concludes that the action of
HUD, including, but not limited to, its environmental impact
statement, comply in all respects with the requirements of
the National Environmental Policy Act of 1969 . . .; the
Federal Guide Lines [sic] of the Council on Environmental
Quality; the Urban Growth and New Community Development
Act of 1970 (Title VII) . . .; and the Water Pollution Prevention and Control Act Amendments of 1972 . . .; and further,
that Title VII is not unconstitutional. [18]

The judge continued, however, to express at great length his concerns
about the aquifer and its potential pollution. While observing that
"the exacting restrictions" placed upon SAR were the only meaningful
attempt so far to control the use of land over the recharge zone, he
also retained jurisdiction of the case to ensure that the safeguards
would indeed be implemented and ordered SAR, the TWQB, and the
EUWD to file reports with the court every six months on the status
and results of all measures utilized at SAR. Further, Judge Spears
credited the plaintiffs with performing a valuable public service in
bringing the suit against SAR, because the suit forced HUD and the
developers to conduct environmental studies and to prepare an adequate
EIS finally, and because the publicity helped alert the citizenry to the
dangers of pollution to the aquifer. In recognition of this service, the
judge then invited the plaintiffs to submit an argument that some of
their attorneys' fees should be paid by the defendants. (The plaintiffs
offered such an argument soon thereafter, and were rewarded with
an order for the SAR developers to pay their attorney fees in an amount
to be determined later; HUD, as a federal government agency, is
immune to such assessments.)[19]

Since no one party was entirely satisfied with the ruling, the
motions and appeals commenced in early June 1973. HUD filed a
motion requesting Judge Spears to delete all references to retention
of jurisdiction and submittal of reports, thus in effect asking the judge
to return full authority over SAR to HUD alone. Spears rejected this
request, stating that it was "highly appropriate for this Court to act
as a central depository to receive all pertinent material available with

respect to any development in the recharge zone of the Edwards Aquifer."[20] At the same time as the ruling, the SAR developers announced that they were "pleased to comply with the court's judgment" and would be making the periodic reports. When the first reports came due on July 1, all parties filed except the TWQB. After a public demand from Judge Spears to show cause for the inaction, the TWQB reluctantly submitted its report.

In July the SAR developers filed a motion with Judge Spears to reconsider his ruling on their reimbursement of the plaintiff attorney fees. This motion was denied at a hearing in August with the award of $20,000 to attorney Hardberger for his efforts in behalf of the plaintiff private organizations (the EUWD and Bexar County opted out of the compensation). Judge Spears declared that these organizations had "lost the case, they lost the battle, but they won the war to protect and save the Edwards Aquifer." He considered his decision "unusual but not out of line."[21]

In early June the four private organizations had decided to appeal Judge Spears' basic decision to permit SAR to proceed with development. They had been quickly joined by the EUWD and Bexar County, although the vote of the Commissioners Court was attended by vigorous opposition to the action from Hayden Head and other SAR supporters. The first move in the appeal was the filing of notice of appeal in the District Court and requesting Judge Spears to enjoin further SAR development activity pending a hearing in the U.S. Fifth Circuit Court of Appeals in New Orleans. Judge Spears ordered SAR and HUD to show cause why such an injunction should not be continued (from prior to the May trial) until the appeal would be heard. On August 21, 1973, at the same time as the ruling on reimbursement of attorney fees for the plaintiffs, Spears refused to grant the injunction, declaring that the SAR developers could proceed with thier plans but "they will do so at their own peril" until the Appeals Court would hear the case.[22]

From that day in court, two separate appeals emanated (joining HUD's appeal of the June refusal to reconsider the court's retention of jurisdiction over SAR). The SAR developers appealed Judge Spears' decision on payment of plaintiff attorney fees. The plaintiff organizations and agencies continued their appeal of the basic decision on SAR development by requesting the U.S. Fifth Circuit Court of Appeals to maintain the status quo on SAR pending a full hearing of the case. The TWQB had decided to join the jurisdiction appeal, but later reversed itself and remained only as defendant-intervenor in the plaintiff appeal. Not until the end of March 1974 did the Appeals Court rule on the new injunction request, once again denying the plaintiffs the stay relief they felt they needed. The full case was argued in May.

The Appeals Court decision was finally handed down on October 4, 1974, over 2 1/2 years from the date the suit was originally filed. The three judges (Wisdom, Clark, and Grooms) found completely for the SAR developers and HUD. The court affirmed the District Court in dismissing all arguments that HUD acted improperly in approving the SAR application:

> The record before us does not support the claim that HUD failed to consider all relevant Title VII factors in reaching its decision or that the decision itself manifests a clear error in judgment.[23]
> . . . the record is clear that the February 23 offer of commitment followed the circulation of the impact statement to the Council on Environmental Quality and other public agencies and groups by more than the specified thirty days.[24]
> There is no NEPA prohibition against . . . a new community applicant providing the federal agency . . . data, information, reports, groundwork environmental studies or other assistance in the preparation of an environmental impact statement.[25]
> It is true that the scope and extent of HUD's treatment of alternatives was less than exhaustive . . . [but it] must be judged against a rule of reason. . . . In this light the statement cannot be condemned for its failure to discuss either the acquisition of the recharge zone as a part at a prohibitive cost, or the elimination of all federal assistance to any development over the recharge zone.[26]
> The project agreement makes it the developer's legally enforceable duty to comply with all present and future environmental quality standards. The developer has agreed to undertake measures to minimize soil erosion and control of sediment and water run-off during the construction phases. To effectuate its duty of quality control and inspection of public improvement construction projects, the developer in conjunction with the City of San Antonio, the Texas Water Quality Board and the Texas State Department of Health has agreed to create an environmental committee, an architectural review board and to employ an independent inspection agent, whose reports will be available to all public and other regulatory agencies. We view the efforts expended to protect the aquifer as substantial and apparently efficacious.[27]
> . . . the developer must act to prevent the Ranch from degrading the existing water quality in the aquifer. If the Ranch is discovered to be polluting the underground water supply, the developer has the legally enforceable duty to remedy the situation.[28]

In addition, the Appeals Court reversed Judge Spears in the two accessory issues of attorneys' fees (appealed by SAR) and retention of jurisdiction (appealed by HUD). In the former, the judges cited precedent for such an award of fees and implied that the present situation was proper for an award, but only against the immune governmental agency HUD for its previously inadequate and noncompliant impact statements.

> In the absence of proof that the private party controlled the governmental agency's actions or caused its default, it cannot be cast in judgment as a result of the agency's shortcomings. The fact that the breach of duty involved was committed by one who is immune from liability for financial redress affords no basis for a shifting of fees. [29]

In the latter issue, the court chastised Judge Spears for his sympathetic retention of jurisdiction over the aquifer development matters (at the expense of HUD's role vis-a-vis SAR).

> The district court must abjure the role of a quasi-administrative agency for environmental affairs in Bexar and other affected counties. No evidence whatever indicates that HUD will fail to discharge faithfully its statutory functions. [30]

The case, with all its findings and orders, was to be remanded to the District Court for proper execution. The plaintiffs pressed another motion for a rehearing in the Appeals Court, but it was summarily denied. This was the end of the road for the long litigation.

## SAR AND THE FUTURE

### Protecting the Aquifer

Although the SAR controversy and litigation were characterized largely by bitterness and divisiveness, in the aftermath can be seen some seeds of positive change that may herald improvements in the future. The major note of optimism generated by the storm of SAR on the community has been the increased attention to safeguarding the purity of the water in the Edwards Aquifer for the future. Even before the SAR trial had begun, the TWQB staff proposed a new Edwards Order of regulations governing development on the recharge zone of the aquifer, to supersede its 1970 order that had proven to be so ineffective. The new order proposed to institute such regulatory features as prohibiting of cesspools, licensing and fees for private sewer systems, and developer-operated monitoring of water quality. To many agencies and organizations in the area this long-awaited revised order was a great disappointment in its limited scope and timid standards and enforcement. Some complained vigorously that stronger measures be implemented, and the TWQB began its usual series of public hearings in the face of opposition from all sides.

Finally, in May 1973, immediately following the SAR trial, AACOG, one of the indignant agencies, formed an Edwards Aquifer Task Force to develop counterproposals for protection of the recharge zone. Composed of representatives of many local and regional agencies, the Task Force commissioned studies and debated policies over several months, ending in September with its own version of an Edwards Order decidedly more restrictive than the official proposal of the TWQB. The Task Force recommendations generally involved greater control over sewer systems, banning certain land uses, and setting of water quality standards for surface streams in the area. The recommendation package was adopted by most of the constituent agencies and forwarded to the TWQB with the force thereof. After more public hearings, the TWQB in March 1974 approved a compromise order which was stronger than the original TWQB staff proposal but not as comprehensive as adopted by the Task Force. The resulting order represented a significant victory for the protectionists, but was still disappointing after the Task Force efforts and expectations.

That there even was such a revised TWQB order can be credited to the SAR imbroglio of several years' duration. After the histrionics died down and the legal actions dwindled, the water quality agencies in the area utilized the heightened sensitivities and level of concern over the aquifer to accomplish some major improvements in protecting the recharge zone and the water supply. SAR was the impetus for initiating any revisions at all, and at every step the restrictions and standards imposed on SAR were the models for application to the balance of the recharge zone.

Late in 1974 the local environmental groups formed an Aquifer Protection Association with the single purpose of raising funds for purchase of land on the recharge zone of the aquifer, finally giving substance to earlier futile dreams of environmentalists and Representative Gonzalez at the height of the SAR furor. Although the goal is distant, some success could be achieved if contributions attract grants and loans, as in similar efforts to save historically cherished structures from demolition. Again, the SAR experience was the key motivating force in this aquifer-protection approach.

Prospects and Prognosis

The future of SAR itself is somewhat clouded. The 30-year development period has been repeatedly moved back as the delays have lengthened. With the conclusion of the litigation and the execution of a project agreement with HUD, the SAR development can finally begin. But the victory may have been somewhat pyrrhic. The prospects for the successful future of SAR have dimmed as the delays have mounted. Developmental competition in the area has stiffened as SAR lost its timing advantage (and missed the first major influx for UTSA). The delays and the extra standards for SAR have increased front-end costs to enormous proportions, but any diminution of facilities or services to cut costs would have to be laboriously negotiated with HUD. Finally, growth prospects themselves have tarnished to some degree, with the arrival of economic recession and less optimistic projections of the population and economy of the future. Additionally, the outlook for far suburban communities may not be so bright with uncertainties in automobile usage and energy availability. The SAR developers and their HUD sponsors may yet wish they had decided to sell out to the "butchers" when they had an opportunity.

While SAR as a real estate development may suffer, the bitter legacy of SAR in local politics will surely be a long time in dying completely. SAR is still a topic of discussion which almost no political figure can address with equanimity. Forces either initiated or accelerated by the SAR controversy in San Antonio have helped usher out a mayor, five city councilmen, a county commissioner, two city managers, and a planning director. Whether or not SAR was uniquely responsible for any of these departures is speculation, but it is clear that San Antonio's once unified political structure has become increasingly fragmented and its power unmanageably diffused. In the aftermath of SAR, the city politics is moving toward more consistent conflict which may undermine the unity common in pre-SAR times.

Finally, the role of SAR in the new communities movement cannot be underestimated. The long struggle dramatically demonstrated the vulnerability of government-backed new communities to virtual destruction by legal action of private and public groups. With troubles from all sides, HUD has now clamped a moratorium on new applications for Title VII assistance. Even so, private developers had been increasingly wary of the Title VII program because of the restrictions and requirements imposed by HUD, many derived from the SAR experience, and the potential for lengthy delays. The developers of one new community (Beckett) even declined the HUD offer of commitment after their application was approved. Although the Title VII program has its currently most serious problems in stabilizing the economics of new communities and in rationalizing federal participation, the lessons from SAR cannot be ignored. The opposition from governments and citizens to all types of new communities has been growing rapidly. Federal agencies and private developers alike will have to adopt new approaches to implementing their projects, and the old procedures will become liabilities. Thus SAR as the first court-tested Title VII new community may end up as the harbinger of the future for many new communities around the country.

## NOTES

1. Source of information was Bexar County Records.

2. For a full treatment of the politics of the UTSA decision, including the relationships among John Connally, Charles Kuper, Alfred Negley, and John Peace, see Ronnie Dugger, Our Invaded Universities: Form, Reform and New Starts (New York: W.W. Norton & Co., Inc., 1974), pp. 282-88; see also "The University of Texas at San Antonio Site Acquisition Study," prepared by John Henson and Stephen M. Vaughan for the Legal Research Project, UT at Austin, September 5, 1971, and the San Antonio Express, May 30, 1970.

3. Office of Management and Budget, Circular A-95 (July 24, 1969); revised (February 9, 1971); revised (November 13, 1973).

4. U.S. Department of Housing and Urban Development, Department Policies, Responsibilities and Procedures for Protection and Enhancement of Environmental Quality, Circular 1390.1 (July 1971); revised (April 1972); revised (December 1972).

5. See Martha Derthick, New Towns In-Town (Washington, D.C.: The Urban Institute, 1972), Chap. 3.

6. Agreement between The City of San Antonio and San Antonio Ranch, Ltd., February 17, 1972, with City of San Antonio Ordinance No. 40397.

7. See "HUD Guarantee of Texas New Town Contingent Upon Water Protection Studies," HUD News, No. 72-131, February 28, 1972.

8. Adrian A. Spears, Order (March 14, 1972), Sierra Club, et al. v. George W. Romney, et al., U.S. District Court, Western District of Texas, San Antonio Division.

9. San Antonio Express, May 9, 1973.

10. San Antonio Express, May 17, 1973.

11. The Texas Observer, July 13, 1973.

12. Texas Legislature, Acts 1971, 62nd Leg., p. 774, ch. 84; Texas Water Code, Title 4, Chap. 54.

13. Texas Legislature, Acts 1973, 63rd Leg.; added Secs. 54.1021, 54.103, 54.109, 54.110, 54.1231, 54.5121 to Texas Water Code, Chap. 54.

14. Adrian A. Spears, Order (March 7, 1973), Sierra Club, et al. v. George W. Romney, et al., U.S. District Court, Western District of Texas, San Antonio Division, p. 1.

15. San Antonio Express, May 4, 1973.

16. The Texas Observer, June 29, 1973.

17. San Antonio Express, May 18, 1973.

18. Adrian A. Spears, Judgment and Order (May 21, 1973), Sierra Club, et al. v. James T. Lynn, et al., U.S. District Court, Western District of Texas, San Antonio Division, p. 1.

19. See Sierra Club v. Lynn, 364 F. Supp. 834 (W.D. Texas, 1973), at pp. 848-49.

20. Ibid., at p. 846.

21. San Antonio Express, August 22, 1973.

22. See Sierra Club v. Lynn, op. cit., at p. 852.

23. Sierra Club v. Lynn, 502 F. 2d 43 (5th Cir., 1974), at p. 57.

24. Ibid., at pp. 58-59.

25. Ibid., at p. 59.

26. Ibid., at p. 62.

27. Ibid., at p. 63.

28. Ibid., at p. 64.

29. Ibid., at p. 66.

30. Ibid.

# 3

## THE POLITICS OF
## SAN ANTONIO RANCH

The case of San Antonio Ranch New Town provides an unusually fertile opportunity for the examination of political processes and decision making at several levels of government. The impact of the private interests on public policy could be felt in the city, county, regional, state, and federal arenas, and stimulated the exercise of certain types of intergovernmental relations. The SAR case affected many individuals and groups, causing some to expend their political resources and others assiduously to avoid as much as possible becoming involved. The time of SAR was also one of great change in politics, at least on the local and federal levels. In sum, SAR can be an excellent case study in many facets of political process, but it has the inherent limitations of a single-issue example in deriving conclusions.

The sections that follow will investigate sequentially the politics of SAR at each level of government, beginning with the City of San Antonio. The emphasis throughout this analysis will be on SAR as an issue for decision making, not peculiarly as a new community. Politics does not always hinge on the type of issue, but more upon the resources involved and the implications foreseen. The special significance of SAR as a new community will be discussed in Chapter 4 of this study.

LOCAL AND REGIONAL POLITICS

A Model of San Antonio Politics

The most salient single feature of San Antonio's political environment has been the racial and ethnic composition of the City's population.

As of 1970, with a total population of 654,153, San Antonio was 52.2 percent Mexican-American, 39.2 percent Anglo-American, and 7.6 percent Negro.[1] The existence of this distribution has to a major degree determined the framework of the political system of the city. In 1952, during a period of rapid growth for the city, especially in Mexican-Americans, a powerful movement of citizens succeeded in the adoption of a new charter, instituting a council-manager form of government. The organization that had zealously promoted the new charter, and its successor, the Good Government League (GGL), became synonymous with the council-manager government, elected the first City Council, and has overwhelmingly dominated the nonpartisan, at-large elections until recently. As in most council-manager cities, the impetus for reform came from the middle and upper classes, the business and economic leadership, mainly Anglo, aiming to redirect the city government toward protection and advancement of their interests instead of the growing ethnic interests. In the typology of Williams and Adrian, the factions concerned with promoting economic growth led the reform, with the support of the conservative faction which desired to maintain only traditional services, to prevent San Antonio from becoming further entrenched as an arbiter government characterized by strong minority veto power in the old-style machine.[2]

The council-manager form of government, as part of civic "reform," is associated with certain definite characteristics in most places where it exists. The structural changes contribute to middle and upper class domination of city politics, because in nonpartisan and at-large elections, private-regarding lower-class voters tend to stay home (lacking a sense of civic duty) since there is no organization to turn them out. Office seekers must rely on business-oriented civic associations and daily newspapers for election, and the costs of at-large campaigning discourage all but the independently wealthy. The city manager, himself a middle-class professional, feels most at home with business leaders. The lack of competitive party organization encourages interest group politics.[3] What is more,

> It is clear that political reforms may have a significant impact in minimizing the role which social conflicts play in decision making. By muting the demands of private-regarding groups, the electoral institutions of reformed governments make public policy less responsive to the demands which arise out of social conflicts in the population.[4]

The GGL has filled the void of power created by the structural reforms, to uphold and to express the interests of the predominantly Anglo, predominantly middle- and upper-class reformers in the new government.

The GGL membership constitutes the power structure in the community and enjoys wide support among most citizens. Taking part in its deliberations are representatives of the city's leading and most influential law firms, bankers and investors, spokesmen for the cattle and oil interest, real estate developers, merchants, manufacturers, Protestant religious leaders, transportation and communications figures, advertising and public relations personnel, retired military officers, minions of the construction and building enterprises, and leaders of important civic and women's organizations. [5]

The GGL has dominated political life in San Antonio for most of the years since the 1952 charter reform. The environment has been excellent for it to flourish. The dependence of San Antonio on the military and defense expenditures and the predominance in the balance of the economic base of local industries have increased centripetal tendencies of the power distribution. The military, and to some extent civilian federal workers, historically have had far less interest in local politics than their private sector counterparts. Removing a substantial segment of the potential leadership of any community leaves a void. In addition, business leaders tend to exert more political influence in communities where businesses are more locally owned, and tend to act as an elite group. [6] San Antonio not only has a relatively smaller total private economy, but also it is relatively higher in its proportion of home-based industries, than most other cities of its size.

Opposition to the GGL has generally been weak and divided, fielding no full slates of opposition candidates for council elections. Only a few well-known individuals challenge the GGL, chiefly because it costs over $30,000 to campaign well in the at-large elections. The GGL has also exhibited a great amount of cooptation—as soon as someone did well against a GGL candidate, his mirror image appeared on the next GGL slate (such as a woman, or a black). The number of Mexican-American candidates fluctuated with discord and activity on the West Side (Mexican-American area). Also, the GGL has constantly reinforced its identification with reform and the council-manager government.

Unity and consensus were the key to GGL success during its heyday. All screening and deliberations for council candidates were closed to the public, and to the bulk of the 3,000 or so GGL members; recommendations by the board of directors brought automatic approval. When a statement was made to the press, it represented a united sentiment. The City Council operated similarly for many years, although its unanimity in public has been deteriorating in recent years. The council met in executive session for debate and dissent prior to its public weekly meeting, in order to encourage consensus. Appointments to and operations of the important independent boards, such as CPSB, CWB, and others, were carried out in similar fashion, creating a monolithic facade of unified power and decision making in a wide range of local affairs. When two independent councilmen were elected in 1969, the whole structure began to become more difficult to maintain. Although the council elected in 1971 was the entire GGL slate, the previous level of unity and closed debate was not regained. Then, three GGL councilmen bolted the ranks prior to the 1973 election and were reelected (one became mayor), while only five of the nine seats were captured by GGL candidates. The GGL by this time had but a shadow of its previous strength on the council.

The other essential underpinning of GGL power has been Anglo domination. The steady increase in the percentage of Mexican-American population in the city was perceived as a direct threat to the consensus politics on which the GGL had thrived since the charter reform. The 1970 Census revealed for the first time an absolute majority for Mexican-Americans in the city. Consequently, in 1972 the GGL City Council authorized, over a great deal of developer opposition, the annexation of some 75,000 persons, overwhelmingly Anglo, into the city. Although the antagonism of many annexed taxpayers helped to decimate the GGL City Council ranks in the 1973 election, the GGL still hoped for long-run survival of its politics through the Anglo annexation.

In San Antonio, the GGL since its formation has been a close approximation of the community power structure so keenly searched for in cities across the country. It will not greatly benefit this study to debate the relative merits of different approaches to community power definition. Several small-scale power studies have been conducted for San Antonio, and the results seem only to correlate highly with the methodology used. Many of the persons named in these studies appear also in the politics of SAR, but many not named also appear. However, as Alford commented:

> The substantive findings of the community power studies are in remarkable agreement. Most studies share the following conclusions.
>
> 1. Public decision making at any specific time occurs within a relatively narrow "agenda of alternatives" determined by constraints of political and economic structure and culture, deriving from the history of the nation, state, and local community.
>
> 2. The middle and upper classes provide most community leadership.

3. When working class groups are organized into politically active unions, a base of opposition to the middle class is created which allows the raising of a variety of issues not usual when only the middle class is active.

4. In particular public decision-making situations, a variety of groups is likely to be active and the same persons are not likely to be found in all issue areas, except for certain public leaders like the mayor or the city manager.

5. At any specific point in time, distinctions concerning the proper boundaries between private and public actions establish the legitimacy of actions by government and public leaders.

6. As a corollary, many major decisions are made autonomously by private economic leaders and are not subject to public control.[7]

Many cities without large, well-organized labor unions as a counterbalance tend to be dominated by the business and economic interests; in general, San Antonio can be said to fall in this category. San Antonio is unusual, however, in having an organization like the GGL that has provided an institutional vehicle for the business and economic interests to affect directly the public decision making. It is no surprise, therefore, that the basic goal for policy of the city has appeared to be that of promoting economic growth.

The dominant elite of San Antonio has been remarkably free of ideology, however. Of the five basic criteria posited by Agger, Goldrich, and Swanson for political ideologies,

- conception of the community
- preferences as to "who shall rule"
- sense of social (socioeconomic) class
- sense of cultural class or caste
- attitudes toward a legitimate method of allocating values[8]

only the second can be considered to be a major concern of the dominant economic group in San Antonio politics, and it for mostly practical purposes. There has been no overall conception of the community, no ideological basis for "who shall rule," no overriding sense of social or cultural class (except to some extent racial and ethnic prejudice), and no systematic attitudes toward a legitimate method of allocating values. The elite of San Antonio are pragmatic in their orientation to public policy, with the objectives of maintenance of power and guiding public policy as necessary to advance the business and economic interests represented. Even with the deterioration of the GGL as the institutional vehicle of the economic elite, a certain amount of consensus on interests manages to set policy directions.

Many groups exist and are active in San Antonio, but they are limited to social, cultural, environmental, or other specific interests that do not impinge on the economic structure or system. Such groups, therefore, form part of the social fabric of the city, but have no way of entering the political arena, regardless of the issue involved. Parenthetically, it might be pointed out that the Mexican-American community has had a structure of social and other interest groups almost parallel to and separate from the Anglo groups, and thus has been nonthreatening even in those activities. The potentially most powerful groups have been the community action and Model Cities organizations formed during the 1960s under direct federal prodding: the city government managed to neutralize one and to absorb the other.

Of the so-called power structure, only a couple of individuals stand out as the preeminent decision makers in San Antonio. Perhaps this situation can be attributed to the ascendancy of the power of organizations rather than individuals, and to the fact that corporate, bank, or real estate affiliations confer power on their leading practitioners. The two men most frequently named in power studies, former Mayor Walter W. McAllister and contractor H.B. Zachry, could even fall into this category, but their influence has been far greater than their positions would indicate. Whether or not the above is true, few Mexican-Americans and fewer blacks are actually included in the so-called power structure, and then only because of elective positions (Gonzalez, Pena), influence over their own people, or membership in the GGL itself. There is little question that the reform has succeeded in keeping control of the San Antonio city government in Anglo hands.

The Case of HemisFair

From 1962 through 1968 San Antonio was in the throes of preparing and hosting a world's fair, the HemisFair of 1968. From inception to postmortem, HemisFair was a series of political issues spanning all the levels of government and the public and private sectors. U.S. Representative Henry B. Gonzalez is generally credited with initiating the governmental and public campaigns for HemisFair, but arrangements and financing were particularly assisted by the presence of two San Antonio area residents in high offices—Lyndon Johnson as President and John Connally as Governor. The dedication of both men to making HemisFair a success left a debt of gratitude in San Antonio that can never be fully repaid.

The legacy of HemisFair is difficult to exaggerate. San Antonio has HemisFair Plaza, the Tower of the Americas, and a convention center where aging houses once stood. But former Senator Ralph Yarborough's reprisals on HemisFair for a double-cross on a Bexar County election perhaps cost him his Senate seat in 1970. The political links forged between local leaders and the Johnson and Connally organizations endure effectively to this day (despite the demise of the chiefs). The work of H.B. Zachry as chairman of the HemisFair executive committee secured for him an almost legendary place in the San Antonio power structure. The other active executive committee members, GGLers almost to the man (or woman), managed to cement places for themselves in the decision-making structure of the city and to augment further both the power and eliteness of the GGL. The disillusionment of the politicking associated with HemisFair, plus the private underwriting losses incurred by hundreds of San Antonians, did much to sour the city on future public-spirited projects. In return, business activity in almost every category received an enormous boost by the construction and retail boom that HemisFair generated. [9]

But at least partially due to the pressures and turmoil created during the course of HemisFair preparation and operation, the consensual politics of the GGL has had great trouble ever since. First was the victory in 1969 of two liberal independents for council seats, a direct effect of the HemisFair disillusionment and losses. But even when the GGL regained full control in 1971, there was not the unity and pragmatism that had been characteristic previously. To be sure, the powerful Mayor McAllister retired in 1971, but the GGL and its political structure were designed around interests, not personalities. By the 1973 election, the gap had become a chasm, as only five GGL candidates for the City Council won seats, and the GGL lost the mayor's position for the first time. In addition, another political citizens' association was formed prior to the election which, while not fielding a complete slate of candidates, did not bode well for continued GGL domination or for future unity and conflict suppression in general.

### The Local Politics of SAR

As a local issue, San Antonio Ranch did not rival HemisFair in any dimension except that of emotion: instead it followed in the wake of HemisFair. In terms of political theory,

> a key issue is one that involves a genuine challenge to the
> resources of power or authority of those who currently

dominate the process by which policy outputs in the system are determined.[10]

Accordingly, HemisFair was a long-standing key issue in San Antonio politics, while SAR was not—at least not until the last months of 1971.

The fact was that, until SAR was revived through the interaction of HUD and Planning Director Davis in October 1971, following the Draft EIS, SAR was not an issue, so far as the City of San Antonio was concerned. Prior to the presentation to the AACOG GARC in March 1971, SAR was only dimly perceived by key decision makers in San Antonio, and was totally unknown to most people. It had been connected with the UTSA site location decision, which surprisingly enough was never much of a major issue in San Antonio, and few leaders even bothered to get involved. SAR was also perceived as just another large subdivision, which was not unusual since local development has been dominated by several large firms, a couple of which were at that time working on sizable "new communities" of their own. Finally, SAR was definitely not seen as an issue symbolizing pollution of the only water supply and diversion of federal funds for the central city.

The AACOG meetings were viewed by the SAR developers as nonthreatening (Honts did not even attend the first GARC session), until the approval was not easily forthcoming. The only real voice of dissent was that of CBE President Char White, who backed down after no support materialized and firm promises were given for an aquifer study group of public agencies. Other committee members equivocated, but no issue was ignited at any level of politics.

The San Antonio power structure did not become involved with SAR until it had been forged into an issue in October 1971. One reason for the noninvolvement was a whole set of mistaken perceptions about SAR. The project was seen as an exercise in wishful thinking or as a large but ordinary subdivision, and not as a major federal funding action nor as high-powered competition for existing developments. SAR was the product of "outside" people—CMH of Austin, Head of Corpus Christi, and others—who, although they had many important San Antonio contacts, had not directly implicated any major local developers or investors. As such, before SAR became an issue San Antonians were too busy with in-fighting to notice the outsiders, but after SAR had become an issue the locals could rally safely against the outsiders. Also, because SAR was not comprehended as a major federal project action, no Mexican-American or black groups were stimulated to raise objections to priorities for a suburban development and thus launch SAR in the political arena as an issue. In addition, since many people in San Antonio considered SAR as "pie-in-the-sky," the environmentally concerned citizens did not at first realize the nature of the threat to the aquifer posed by SAR. These groups had not addressed the aquifer protection problem as yet, and thus were quite unprepared to evaluate SAR.

A second set of reasons for the early noninvolvement of the power structure revolved around the unwritten developmental policy in San Antonio. With the substantial presence of real estate and construction interests in the GGL and its elected and appointed positions, the basic policy on land development then existing was one of strong laissez-faire. All potential public developmental controls, such as zoning, subdivision review, roads, and utilities, were automatically granted or sold upon the initiative of the private developer. Thus if the private sector wished to develop a parcel of land, the public (that is, the City of San Antonio) would support it. This phenomenon has been called a "system of private government" for the housing industry.[11] The GGL development interests were willing to grant this to the SAR developers as those interests would have for themselves. This type of policy represents the "mobilization of bias" identified by Schattschneider: "Some issues are organized into politics while others are organized out."[12]

Overall, the silence of the decision leaders of San Antonio on the SAR matter, prior to October 1971, can be attributed to lack of information and the operation of the existing mobilization of bias on developmental matters. Wolfinger called this the nonparticipation form of nondecision making:

> . . . situations in which people are unaware of their interests and therefore do not demand that those interests be served. This unconscious non-decision-making is said to be due to values and procedures that set limits on the community agenda of issues.[13]

But when the matter of SAR received the impetus to arrive at center stage and become an issue, it could not be dealt with in the nondecision framework. The rapid-fire sequence of no-gos, in City Manager Henckel's wire and in the Planning Commission and the City Council positions, conferred on SAR the status of "issue." The snowballing effect of the media coverage, the declared opposition of other public officials, and the emergence into action of civic and environmental groups, all countered by vast amounts of pressure from the SAR side, converted an ordinary issue into a key issue. As a key issue, it represented a genuine threat to the existing distribution of power and mobilization of bias, thus forcing the chief decision makers of the city into action.

SAR was so little an issue in October 1971 when it exploded through City Council that even the pro and con arguments regarding it were not very well established. These were supplied by Davis and the Planning Department. The con that Henckel accepted was the adverse fiscal impact on the city. The Planning Commission saw 90,000 people being siphoned off from other local developments. The City Council picked on the financial impact and the competition for funds arguments. SARA and EUWD, naturally, worried about aquifer pollution hazards as did most of the involved private organizations. Each party landed on a different point of objection to SAR, but this situation only allowed a great deal of opposition to form quickly and to be perceived as a united front. In contrast, SAR was caught by surprise, had no effective counters to all arguments on short notice, and needed time to mobilize its political resources to work through the elite decision-making structure of the city.

At the time of the moratorium, the fast pace of events slackened and the SAR counteroffensive began. CMH does not claim to be a development firm: "We're politicians, not regular developers." CMH, as head of the SAR development team, had three objectives at this point: (1) to get the City Council back to a neutral position and out of its negative stance; (2) to form a truce with Mayor Gatti—a chance to talk peaceably; and (3) to neutralize the newspaper coverage.

The tactics were manifold and very straightforward. Every major protagonist in the debate, including every councilman, was visited, lobbied, cajoled, and promised, sometimes more than once, by Bob Honts, Hayden Head, or a deputy, accompanied by an appropriate acquaintance. These visits permitted the SAR side to counter each argument head-on, and to offer or threaten sanctions as necessary. These confrontations provided the communication through which direct power relationships were established and utilized.[14]

The above tactics were the most visible, but perhaps not the most effective. According to the model of San Antonio politics, the best strategy for achieving all three objectives would be to actuate the power elite. This was attempted in several ways. Two mid-level but active economic leaders and GGLers, car dealer Red McCombs and developer William Ochse, were enlisted as associates for CMH, to be cut in as prime investors in a fancied new town in-town. The presence of McCombs and Ochse really turned the tide toward the accomplishment of the CMH objectives. Both were active in the Chamber of Commerce (Ochse a recent past president), which was composed of the cream of the GGL business underpinnings. McCombs and Ochse were able to activate the mostly neutral businessmen in the Chamber. The Chamber credo of supporting anything that would bring new dollars into San Antonio was easily invoked and won many easy SAR backers. These in turn worked wonders in the banking, corporate, and development sectors in rallying support for SAR.

The types of messages carried through these channels of communication seemed to be that SAR could be a positive economic attribute for San Antonio, and that a minority of liberal do-gooders were attempting to derail a legitimate private enterprise. The effects were quick and clear. The newspaper coverage died immediately. The Light, with publisher Frank Bennack linked to the developers, had never reported much on the SAR furor, after an earlier, highly laudatory series on SAR and new towns in general. But the Express-News, which had been spearheading the making of SAR as an issue, suddenly stopped publishing anything on SAR. As it turned out, this halt was due to several factors. Honts had been threatening reporter Deborah Weser with reprisals for her antagonistic journalism, but had not been able to make the threats stick. Now the pressure hit Express-News publisher Charles Kilpatrick (probably through the then owner Houston Harte), and the newspapers rapidly reevaluated their policy on SAR coverage. But at the same time Honts' frenetic activity around the city had caused the previously fertile news and quote sources to dry up.

It was a simple matter of light pressure through the city council to get the city manager to muffle the city staff, especially Davis and the Planning Department, whose professional efforts had helped build the issue. The same light pressure applied through the Executive Committee guaranteed staff silence from AACOG. The Chamber of Commerce network also tried to reach other staff opposition in SARA and EUWD through the board members, but with success as limited as Honts' in his personal appeals. Few of those board members were San Antonians (SARA and EUWD extend over several counties); those that were local were independently elected and thus were not as closely tied to GGL and Chamber interests as were appointed city boards such as Urban Renewal, CPSB, and CWB. Attempts were also made on the private opposition, but with little success, since the members of those groups represented much of the long-standing political opposition to the GGL anyway.

But the strongest and most consistent pressures were exerted on the city councilmen, whose withdrawal of the no-go was the major objective. The most important member of the council was one that never changed his position—Mayor John Gatti. He had been off the council for two years prior to being asked by the GGL to run as its candidate for mayor to replace departing Mayor McAllister. An investment broker by occupation, Gatti had long been an important functionary in the GGL, but was not a member of the socioeconomic elite so powerful in city affairs. In becoming mayor he attempted to chart his own course in certain matters to distinguish him and his administration from that of McAllister. To this end Gatti strove to identify himself with the redevelopment of the downtown and central city, among other things. The SAR proposal, when it arrived before City Council in October 1971, was perceived as particularly antithetical to the funding of this redevelopment, especially a new town in-town solution. Gatti came down hard on the side of the opposition to SAR, and never wavered, despite incredible pressure from the developers, other councilmen, and many business leaders in the city who had supported his election through the GGL. Gatti reacted by trying to insulate himself from the raging storm; he ended up listening to his colleagues and backers, but refused even to grant an audience to Honts and his whirlwind lobbying show.

Of the other councilmen, Charles Becker, an ardent advocate of the economic growth philosophy and clearly committed to suburban development over inner city with his Handy Andy locational policy, crossed to the SAR side early in the struggle. He became a valuable ally for the developers because of his influence over the Garza-Mendoza-Naylor bloc in the council, as well as on account of his power in the business community and GGL. Garza responded easily to this and to Zachry's persuasion, while Naylor was successfully lobbied as real-estate-to-real-estate interests. Mendoza was flexible enough to see the advantages of not being stubborn, plus reacting favorably to hints of support for his pet project of a West Side stadium. Haberman received strong and meaningful pressure through her husband—then general manager of Ochse's St. Anthony Hotel (he later resigned for a similar position at another hotel). Ed Hill also changed, but the reasons are not clear. Most of the council attended a SAR developer-sponsored hunting weekend during the critical weeks of decision, and at least one of the wavering members was finally won over at that intensive "briefing" session.

Besides Gatti, the other two negative votes on SAR on the City Council were based on cynicism of minority groups. Felix Trevino subscribed to the argument of "only so much Fed money in the pot," meaning the competition for federal funds between SAR and other areas of San Antonio. In addition, he felt that SAR, despite its claims, would not help low-income people. Dr. Robert Hilliard had been given a special SAR presentation by Honts at the St. Anthony Hotel, since he had missed the November Council presentation. Hilliard would not budge under the pressure because of his concerns for inner city funding and the aquifer. When he told Honts that he would not change, Honts stated the SAR goal of a unanimous council vote in favor of SAR as ammunition in the lawsuit he suspected lay in the future.

When the City Council finally voted 6-3 for SAR in December 1971, and again in February 1972, it signified a milestone in the openness of the bitterness and the divisions on the council. During the course of the debate the scope of the political issue had been enlarged from that of a development matter with environmental overtones to that of a major power play involving the integrity of the GGL and the policy of unrestricted private initiative. The arena changed from technical staff review (AACOG A-95 and Planning Department comments on the Draft Environmental Impact Statement) to citywide interest (actually only civic-minded or public-regarding citizens). Thus SAR was removed from the narrow nonelectoral politics of interested groups and individuals, in which the GGL and its mobilization of bias operate best, to a more open arena with electoral implications. As participation in the issue increased, so did the chances of the SAR opponents.[15]

On SAR, cleavages in the GGL ranks appeared on a nonpolicy issue where they traditionally had not shown. This phenomenon is not characteristic of the consensual, in-group politics that the GGL had represented for two decades. A strong campaign by certain business leaders stimulated by Honts and Christian, McCombs and Ochse eventually won the approval for SAR, but it perhaps was a pyrrhic victory with a bitter legacy even within the GGL power structure itself. In the SAR case, certain indications of a different style of politics could be glimpsed, perhaps an emerging model for San Antonio, as well as other cities. It has been called New Politics to distinguish it from the brokerage and the reform styles. The New Politics is characterized by elements appearing in regard to the SAR issue: the arena of political conflict is enlarged, there is increasing intensity to political struggles and issues, more actors (individuals and groups) participate in politics, and governmental actions are increasingly questioned on grounds of legitimacy.[16]

The appearance on the political scene of militant environmentalist groups (as well as more militance from older civic organizations) forebodes further widening of the conflicts. This movement in San Antonio really began with the opposition of the San Antonio Conservation Society to the North Expressway during the 1960s (leading through a lawsuit to the Supreme Court in 1970). The Conservation Society is composed chiefly of active women belonging to the socioeconomic elite of San Antonio. Militance from a source such as this against clear policy positions of the City Council, the GGL, and the majority of business and economic interest could only encourage greater political participation by other groups and individuals, to the detriment of closed, nonelectoral politics. In one sense, most of the groups attracted to militant opposition represent single-interest and long-standing anti-GGL members whose activity constitutes no new threat to consensual elite politics. But more and more the groups are attracting the interest and allegiance of solid middle-class citizens who have been the mainstay of the GGL. The issues that such groups are and will be addressing, like SAR, are very likely to be in policy areas of economic growth and development long taken for granted by the GGL.

The bitter split on the GGL City Council over SAR, however, may have been just another in a series of issues leading to cleavages in the ranks. At least two different factions, roughly headed by Gatti and Becker, had been forming almost since the April 1971 elections. Although it was partially a power play (Gatti to solidify, Becker to acquire), one of the central issues had been identified by other councilmen as concerning the publicly owned, but independent, utilities—CPSB, CWB, and San Antonio Transit System. Gatti wanted to reform the utilities within the existing independent structure, while Becker favored a more complete overhaul including, if necessary, elimination of the boards. Such a move would strike hard at the core of the structure of consensual politics in effect for so many years. The utility boards provided the mechanism for the intimate involvement of the GGL elite in all city affairs (on a part-time basis) with self-perpetuation through a closed appointment system. Becker, on the other hand, apparently saw political domination best maintained through centralization of power in the City Council and mayor.

By the time of the election campaign of 1973, the GGL could not hide cracks appearing in its once-solid core. Becker and two other GGL councilmen (Padilla and Mendoza, the latter at the last possible minute) bolted the GGL to run as part of an independent slate of candidates. The GGL selection board had a difficult time in finding strong candidates to seek election under its banner. The lackluster slate won five of nine places, but allegiances were so low that one GGLer voted with the minority to elect Becker mayor. Once seated, this divided council could be characterized as special-interest-oriented, argumentative, and dilatory, unable to grasp or to act on policy issues. The inactivity and the breakdown of the fine-tuned consensus opened the political arena more and more to outside interests, creating a chaotic situation, which is likely to lead to some changes in the council-manager and electoral systems set up in 1952 (especially at-large elections, the bane of activist minority groups).

The role of SAR in the larger picture of council politics apparently was to exacerbate existing cleavages. The time it appeared was a turning-point for GGL consensus politics, but whether SAR was a prime cause, another contributing element, or an effect is difficult to determine. In any case it was a key political issue and very likely causative to some extent.

Later in the SAR history, U.S. Representative Henry B. Gonzalez demonstrated his continued potency in state and local politics, as well as in intergovernmental politics. Gonzalez, a major force in the HemisFair preparations, was unusually silent throughout most of the SAR controversy. A well-known liberal of the 1950s, as councilman and state representative, he had first been elected to Congress with the active support of then Vice President Johnson. His politics matured into a pragmatic and flexible synthesis of domestic liberalism and foreign hawkishness. In recent elections he has been unopposed for reelection in his district. Always unpredictable, Gonzalez normally maintains close surveillance of the local San Antonio scene, intervening strongly on particular issues with his considerable political clout. His influence seems to stem chiefly from his long-term political relationships, his ubiquitous presence, his links to federal funds, his selection of issues, and his vehemence on the offensive. A local political axiom that surfaced again during the new town in-town period admonishes: "Don't cross swords with Zorro, don't try to unmask the Lone Ranger, and don't mess around with Henry B. Gonzalez."[17]

Gonzalez remained neutral during most of the SAR political conflict, but intervened strongly and decisively in the matters of the SANT and the MUD for SAR in 1973. His effect was greatest on the state legislature, where he helped defeat the SANT urban renewal law changes and promoted the MUD amendments. Overall, the role of Gonzalez is difficult to assess with respect to political models, but he remains a powerful and active force in San Antonio (and congressional) politics, and seemingly independent of all contending factions.

The case of SAR also represents another major intrusion of a federal program into San Antonio. The city, of course, has been familiar with military programs and personnel for many years, but (as has been described) the military and Defense Department officials have discreetly avoided local politics for the most part. San Antonio received its first large taste of politicized federal programs in the 1960s with the antipoverty and Model Cities agencies. These caused innumerable political problems for the City Council because they stirred up quiescent minority groups and owed financial allegiance to Washington, not to City Hall. To a lesser extent, urban renewal and new communities fall into the same category of public actions independent of the city and its politics.

The implications of an increasing number of federal programs for elite consensus politics are great:

> Individuals in the system, either elite or non-elite, who have some of their needs provided outside the system, may develop competing allegiances and alternative values. Outside contacts offer new means for obtaining goals, new goals, and new models of behavior. External contacts thereby loosen elite controls wherever they exist. . . .
> The legal relationships between the local, state and Federal governments in the United States, as well as the informal political connections emanating from these arrangements, break down the system autonomy necessary for attainment of false consensus. . . . The preservation of

elite consensus and local autonomy depends partially upon
the extent to which demographic, ecological, and socio-
logical characteristics of the community can be controlled.[18]

The involvement and the actions of the SAR developers and HUD officials during the SAR controversy in San Antonio probably hastened the
demise of the system autonomy in San Antonio in which the GGL elite
domination could germinate and perpetuate itself.

Further federal incursions have occurred since SAR. The proposed new town in-town (SANT) was the most important of these.
Sponsored by the same group as is developing SAR, and including
local investors McCombs and Ochse and consultant Pepe Lucero, it
was generally conceded among public officials interviewed that SANT
was conceived and introduced to divert attention from SAR and to
establish some legitimacy and credibility for the SAR developers on
the local scene. Hayden Head admitted to the image-building objective
during a presentation of the proposal to City Council. The developers
approached the ultimate legitimizer, former Mayor McAllister, to
join the new town in-town, but he declined (McAllister was behind
another multimillion dollar downtown project).

Although everyone was in favor of the new town in-town, and no
one opposed, the council and the GGL were again cornered on this
proposal. With the solid backing of HUD, the developers could put any
public official or private business leader on the spot by demanding
acquiescence in a project conceived outside of the policy-making structure of San Antonio which would divert all downtown and river-corridor
urban renewal funding to that site and that project for many years.
The council had gone on record designating the East Side as top priority
for Neighborhood Development Program (NDP) funds, but had to renege
because of SANT. Although the entire river corridor was being planned
as an single entity at the council's direction, all the NDP funds there
would apply to the new town in-town.

The manner of approach by Honts and the other developers to both
proponents and opponents of SAR in seeking endorsement for the SANT
was also uncontrollable. Opponents were read statements of theirs
from the SAR conflict in which they had called for a new town in-town.
They could not very well refuse to endorse this one now. Those who
had been favorable to SAR were also to comment on a take-it-or-
leave-it basis on the new town—to say no would have been to oppose
downtown redevelopment. The analogy was made between these contacts and "sitting ducks."

Initiated and killed outside of San Antonio politics, the new town
in-town thus never became an issue, but its very existence posed a
further implied threat to the elite domination of San Antonio politics.
In one respect, the matter of community power seems to be returning

to a question, not of "who runs the city?" but of "does anyone run the city?"[19] No power structure is stable over time, as the academic elitist scholars imputed. It is likely that the San Antonio elite domination is evolving toward a more multifaceted structure in which false consensus is more difficult to obtain. There will be more interested groups and individuals affecting policy decisions because there will be more levers to pull and more strings attached. Environmentalists can now block projects almost interminably through legal channels; they and others will be making demands earlier in the policy-making process. The federal presence, through revenue sharing and community development block grants, may be more subtle, but the increased funds for local use will produce more diverse constituencies with interests in local politics. However, well-organized groups, such as the homebuilders and real estate interests, which in the past have worked effectively through the GGL, will also be strong, but with more to contend with. In general, conflict will be more the rule than the exception in San Antonio, with wider participation, greater potential rewards, and less directed community objectives. As such, SAR provided valuable insights into a changing political scene in San Antonio.

Bexar County Politics and SAR

County government in Texas manages to combine some of the flavor of the big city political machine with the functions of a small town. Due to the dispersed and fragmented nature of the state government, the county administrative functions have not grown and modernized as they might have. But politics is bigtime and partisan. In most urban counties, such as Bexar, the government is presided over by an elected county judge, who together with four elected commissioners forms the Commissioners Court. The clerk, recorder, treasurer, and district attorney are also elected. All are elected to four-year terms of office. Since civil service is nonexistent or new in most counties, there is plenty of patronage for the elected officials to dispense.

In Bexar County, the Commissioners Court has for a long time been divided between liberal Democrats, conservative Democrats, and a Republican. Albert A. Pena had been the mainstay of the liberal Democrats in the County until his defeat in 1972. He had opposed the GGL on the city level, and, in turn, the GGL supported candidates against him in the county. The biggest GGL coup was the 1966 defeat of Judge Charles Grace, a liberal Democrat, by its candidate, present Judge Blair Reeves, aided by Governor Connally, Mayor McAllister

70

(a Republican), and the Republican Party.[20] Of the others, Frank Vaughan, Republican, and A.J. Ploch, Democrat, a 26-year veteran, had both worked with the GGL, and Tom Stolhandske was a compatible newcomer.

Reeves was quite active in real estate in suburban areas, and had owned land near the UTSA site in northwest Bexar County. He was quite prodevelopment, both because of personal activity and because of benefits to the County tax rolls. Thus, when his friend John Peace introduced Hayden Head to him with a glowing description of the benefits of the SAR project, Reeves was pleased to write his famous letter of endorsement for SAR in March 1971, read to the AACOG GARC meeting. By the time the subject of SAR was revived at the city level, his growing concern for the aquifer (as well as advice from Mayor Gatti) had prompted a change of heart, and he led the Commissioners Court in their November resolution opposing all development on the aquifer. His earlier letter had been written as county judge, but had no authority behind it since the county had not been approached for endorsement and had no official need to be so.

Commissioner Pena was against SAR from the start, for both environmental and locational reasons, although he had no opportunity to voice opposition until the November resolution. He was a member of the AACOG Executive Committee, and moved at the December meeting to rescind the favorable review given SAR the previous May. This motion was the occasion of the close 9-8 vote not to reconsider. Pena and Reeves led the Commissioners Court into the environmentalists' suit against SAR, joined by Ploch.

Ploch was the enigma of the anti-SAR commissioners. He was not much concerned about environmental hazards, but was strictly a Southsider and was still angry about Northside interests "stealing" the UTSA site. Vaughan claimed to oppose SAR, but opposed entry into the suit because he believed that the county had no business taking any position on SAR until requested to do so. Stolhandske was close to the Ben Barnes/Connally wing of the Democratic Party, and apparently was lobbied into support for SAR by George Christian, Barnes' public relations manager and SAR partner.

The Commissioners Court demonstrated considerable independence in its resolution and close vote to join the suit against SAR. Pressures were applied to the commissioners, especially to Reeves and Stolhandske, although without the full hounding that City Council members had received. Reeves, a protege of the GGL, withstood the most influence (from the GGL and the Barnes/Connally group) to ally himself with Gatti on the minority side of the GGL on the SAR question. His concern for the protection of the aquifer was genuine, and he regretted his earlier hasty endorsement. Reeves has since been very active in meetings and other efforts to preserve water quality in Bexar County.

Ted Butler, the district attorney, who by law represents the Commissioners Court in legal actions, was against joining the environmentalist suit against SAR from the start (together with his assistant Yates). Butler condemned the vote to join the suit, claiming the state was an implicit defendant in the case, through the TWQB approval of SAR. He recommended withdrawal from the suit. Although this advice was not heeded, some observers believed that Butler's action was taken not because of the legal ambiguity but because the SAR developers or supporters had "talked to him." In any event, he was not expected to, and in fact did not, pursue the county role in the suit with great alacrity. Later, in October 1972, the SAR attorneys attempted to force the county to withdraw from the suit by claiming to Judge Spears that the county could not legally be represented by private counsel (reference to the environmentalists' attorney Hardberger), but only by the district attorney. Butler then assigned an assistant district attorney (ultimately Burris) to the case and generally supported his enthusiastic efforts for the plaintiffs throughout the litigation.

The county politics is still linked closely with the city's, despite the independence shown by the Commissioners Court on SAR. Several commissioners and other officials are allied with the GGL, although the county is less of an autonomous system than the city and the policy payoffs of control are fewer. But the diminution of GGL unity and control in the city cannot help but free elected county officials to be more independent or to seek other ties.


AACOG and SAR


The legitimacy and significance of AACOG as a political entity rests almost entirely on its designation as the regional clearinghouse for federal actions under Circular A-95, known as the A-95 review process. Under this authority, AACOG has a delegated legal function of reviewing federal projects in the region, including proposed new communities.[21] Its Government Applications Review Committee (GARC) operates as a subcommittee to the Executive Committee, which is composed mostly of elected officials from throughout the eleven-county (now twelve) region. The GARC consists chiefly of professional and administrative persons of various sorts.

The politics of AACOG takes place within the context of the committees, particularly the Executive Committee, but relates mostly to each member's home political environment. Since many of the members are not from Bexar County, this situation creates a very diffused political climate, except for the few Bexar County representatives, for whom AACOG is an extension of city and county politics.

Consequently, in the matter of SAR the AACOG debates and votes were like microcosms of city and county deliberations. In May 1971 the Executive Committee approved SAR with little dissent (although many questions had been raised in the GARC), but in December the committee narrowly defeated a move to reconsider the favorable review. The AACOG staff was mixed in its attitudes toward SAR in the spring, but overwhelmingly against it in the fall, reflecting staff concerns in the city. Although AACOG was at times a significant forum for politicking on SAR (it alone brought together HUD officials, Yantis of the TWQB, other state and regional and city and county officials), it did not surface with a politics of its own, except in terms of potential clout with HUD on project review. Thus the politics of AACOG is perhaps best considered in the context of its constituent agencies and governmental bodies.

## The Regional Agencies: SARA and EUWD

Both SARA and EUWD have a wide geographical coverage: SARA over the entire San Antonio River Basin in Bexar, Wilson, Karnes, and Goliad counties, and EUWD over a full five-county area encompassing most of the Edwards Aquifer. Their elected boards of directors, therefore, have majority composition from outside of Bexar County. Their offices and staffs are located in San Antonio, however, thus focusing a disproportionate amount of activity in Bexar County. Both agencies were established by the state primarily to promote water quality (and for SARA flood control), but most of their regulatory authority was superseded by the TWQB when it was created in 1967. SARA and EUWD can monitor and study water quality, and bring suit against violators of regulations, but must follow the TWQB orders.

The necessarily close working relationship between these agencies and the TWQB was an important factor when SAR became an issue for them. The staffs of SARA and EUWD, headed by Fred Pfeiffer and Colonel McDonald Weinert, respectively, were quite antagonistic towards the SAR proposal, mainly because of the potential pollution hazards. Neither manager was consulted until after the AACOG review in May 1971. Pfeiffer had been present for one of the GARC sessions, and one SARA director, Thomas Drought, was on the Executive Committee. Hugh Yantis of the TWQB briefed Weinert on SAR in June after the review was completed, eliciting from him an endorsement based on promises that TWQB would ensure no pollution. Later, Pfeiffer was also quoted as amenable to SAR.

When SAR burst open as a hot issue in October, however, both managers became vehemently opposed to SAR, and pushed their boards to resolve likewise. Both boards passed resolutions opposing subsidized development on the recharge zone of the aquifer. But the SAR developers then launched a campaign to pressure the directors to return at least to neutral positions. Hayden Head made most of the visits to the directors of both agencies, asking them to change their positions, promising that studies of the aquifer would be conducted and claiming that it could not be proven that SAR would indeed pollute the water supply.

On the SARA board, the pressure was effective. Although Drought, Paul Herder, and a few of the downriver county directors held fast and prevented any outright endorsement of SAR, the SARA board declined to oppose SAR specifically, and was never considered likely to join the environmental suit against SAR. Joining the plaintiffs in the suit, moreover, would have presented great problems for SARA in its normal working relationship with the TWQB (in sewer plant operation). The EUWD board, however, was not deterred by Head's lobbying. It continued unanimously with an authorization to take legal action and then with a resolution to join the environmental suit against SAR, along with financial support therefor.

Both of these regional agencies are embroiled in their own politics, rather minor and independent in perspective. Their actions, however, contributed in a small way to the political dynamics of the SAR case in providing fuel to the conflagration when it was at its most explosive. The efforts of the staffs were important in that they added further professional voices and comments for HUD and the developers to rebut. Further, these agencies and their staffs, especially SARA, were respected within the San Antonio community, and thus their positions had persuasive power. The EUWD provided valuable support for the plaintiffs in the suit against SAR, lending more credibility to the case as a public body entering. Finally, SARA and EUWD were the only vociferous public agencies attending the WQARB meetings in April-June 1972 who challenged the proceeding and the study findings. Thus, while their independent political roles were relatively minor, SARA and EUWD both contributed significantly to the overall politics surrounding the SAR controversy.


## STATE POLITICS


### Cronyism


Texas politics is a wonderful fraternity of monied interests that has webs of relationships and associations that cross party lines but not ideological barriers. The dominant philosophy of this wealth is conservative, yet pinned to economic growth, regardless of whether it is oil, cattle, corporate, or land money. The network of kinship and friendship is so extensive, weaving throughout public and private life, that it could almost be said to constitute an informal government for Texas. People included in the group, and those aspiring to join, utilize the network for critical business and governmental deals and to ensure compliance of the necessary governmental authorities.

At the center of this network are the operatives formerly associated with Lyndon B. Johnson, now mostly on their own. Former governor and Treasury Secretary John Connally falls into this category, as does George Christian, formerly press secretary for both Connally and LBJ, and now head of Christian, Miller, and Honts, developers of SAR (and who consulted first with Connally before committing CMH to SAR). These men are political pragmatists who are utilizing and selling influence that they have acquired within the Texas in-group. During 1972 Christian was busy selling Ben Barnes for governor and Richard Nixon for president, while the previous year he had been selling SAR to HUD and to San Antonio. Meanwhile, Hayden Head, a Republican, was pushing for his old friend Senator Tower, as well as for Nixon, and for SAR. Both were among the elite Texans invited to Connally's ranch not far from San Antonio for barbecues with President Nixon. Judge Adrian Spears, who presided over the SAR trial in U.S. District Court, was a long-time political confrere of LBJ before his appointment to the federal bench. And James U. Cross, then Executive Director of the Texas Parks and Wildlife Department and a member of the TWQB, was LBJ's personal pilot of Air Force One, the presidential jet. The list could continue ad infinitum.

The links extend deeply into San Antonio, too. Connally has been associated with many important San Antonians, but especially with John Peace, former chairman of the University Board of Regents, and Alfred Negley, who, along with Connally, benefited substantially from the UTSA site location decision. Connally's defection to Nixon and later to full Republicanism carried many San Antonio supporters with him. McCombs and Ochse were among the newer breed of Republicans in the area, while former Mayor McAllister and SAR attorney Seagal Wheatley were long-time Republican stalwarts. The GGL and the elite of San Antonio, however, generally fit the conservative Democratic mold once presided over by Connally and his group. The one who defies classification is Representative Gonzalez, a one-time GGL leader and a beneficiary of his association with LBJ, but now a master political pragmatist who belongs to no clique.

The SAR development team had strategic connections to all the centers of power. It was intimately a part of the Texas crony network. It had impeccable Democratic credentials to bring to bear in San

Antonio and Austin, as well as the Republican clout to focus on Washington. This political firepower certainly was a key factor in mobilizing the GGL elite when necessary in San Antonio, as well as indicating the pressure points to aim for on the local and regional level for maximum effectiveness. In Washington, under the Nixon Administration, few proposals were funded unless accompanied by Republican calling cards and promising Republican benefits. The New Communities Program was no exception, and the SAR developers were prepared with Republicans and promises, and had Connally there to plug them in.

The chief inference to be drawn from the SAR case is that Texas still functions in an oligarchic manner, but without the formal elite in public office. The governors since Connally (Preston Smith and Dolph Briscoe) have not been members of this group, but have bowed to its operation. The old LBJ machinery may be dwindling, but the big money interests still program state activity. These interests are of such paramount concern that even a "reform" governor like Briscoe can easily serve them with impunity. The state cronyism has been much less visible than the San Antonio GGL, but has been no less effective in terms of policy outputs. The effects on agenda-setting for the state are quite strong, narrowing the range of decisions for the state government, and to some extent for local governments, to an extremely slender set of choices. Although the network is informal, it has produced the necessary "false" consensus and has suppressed conflict to an amazing degree.

Texas State Government

In general, the state government can be considered to be relatively weak. In most studies of state governments, Texas ranks near the bottom in terms of structure, function, and techniques, indicating a government somewhat retarded in its development. The governor's office is weak, with many appointments to be dispensed, but no budgetary, administrative, initiative, or recall powers assigned to it over operating agencies. A dynamic governor can to some extent overcome these handicaps to become an effective executive. Governor Smith did not achieve this status during his four years in office, and Governor Briscoe, elected in 1972 in the aftermath of petty scandals in the state government, has seemed content with ceremonial functions.

The legislature is quite ordinary as state legislatures go, but lacks the leadership needed to put together total programs. The lieutenant governor is inordinately powerful because of the gubernatorial impotence, but he is really only a glorified legislative whip. Biennial sessions, low pay, high-pressure lobbying, constant in-fighting, and corruption prevent the legislature from preparing and passing much needed legislation in such areas as land development and water pollution.

The day-to-day business of state government is carried out by a very large number of administrative agencies—some 140 at last count. Many of the agencies are headed by part-time boards and commissions which appoint an executive director to run the agency. The governor appoints the boards, but cannot remove them. As a consequence, all of them are virtually independent of the governor, of the legislature (except when they need a bill passed or killed), and of each other. There is a minimum of cooperation among agencies, and a lack of planning and coordination to deal with problems. Isolation from gubernatorial and legislative politics is really only substituted by agency politics. The boards and staffs cannot expect the governor to look out for their interests, so they mobilize their own support among legislators, lobbyists, and client groups. The concerns of these politics are mostly nonelectoral—in influencing specific legislation, in benefiting groups in return for support, and in increasing agency power or jurisdiction.[22]

The foregoing brief discription of state government serves to highlight the context in which SAR came to exist, and to suggest why the state government had a limited role. The TWQB was involved from the start. The Division of Planning Coordination of the governor's office, the closest approximation to a real planning department in the state government, endorsed SAR very early in an almost perfunctory manner, without any responsibility for review and hinging only on A-95 approval. Several other endorsements trickled in, from a local Highway Department office and from the Parks and Wildlife Department (from Executive Director Cross). Later, several more agencies were involved in the WQARB meetings. But, except for the TWQB, no state agency was requested to assume an important role with respect to SAR, and none other was statutorily bound to do so. Consequently, the next section will focus analytically on the relationship between the TWQB and SAR.

The TWQB and SAR

The TWQB was created under the Texas Water Quality Act of 1967, as another quasi-independent board of the state government. The TWQB is charged with maintaining quality of water in Texas for public health and enjoyment, promoting development of regional waste collection, treatment, and disposal systems, and implementing and enforcing the Act.[23] The TWQB consists of three appointees of the Governor and four ex officio members. The chairman at the time of the SAR approvals was Gordon Fulcher (now deceased), a Connally appointee who in private life was the conservative publisher of the *Texas Star* magazine. The ex officio members include the executive directors of the Texas Water Development Board and the Parks and Wildlife Department, the State Commissioner of Health, and the Chairman of the Texas Railroad Commission.[24] The Executive Director chosen by the TWQB is Hugh C. Yantis, Jr.

In 1970 the TWQB issued its original Edwards Order, establishing certain regulations governing development on the recharge areas of the Edwards Aquifer. That order instituted requirements for licensing of all septic tanks located in the recharge areas, and imposed a limitation on residential densities there. Perhaps more important than the substance of the order was the recognition that it gave to the special status of the recharge zone as a critical environmental area.[25] But the 1970 order did not treat the underlying policy issue of whether and how much urban development should occur on these critical areas. This was the issue that surfaced when SAR was being argued on environmental grounds during late 1971.

Chiefly as a result of the SAR controversy, the TWQB passed an amended Edwards Order in March 1974 after a lengthy series of public hearings throughout the Edwards Aquifer region. What was finally adopted was a compromise regulation, less stringent than that advocated by AACOG's Edwards Task Force, but more restrictive than the TWQB staff recommendations. Essentially, the 1974 order banned cesspools, forced licensing and inspection of all new private sewage systems, instituted a process requiring approval by the TWQB of all new subdivisions on the recharge zone, and set some quality standards for effluent discharges. Although it was an improvement, it still did not address basic development issues and left in doubt certain enforcement questions.

The TWQB is considered by many San Antonians not to have lived up to its original promise regarding protection of the aquifer. As weak as it was, the 1970 Edwards Order was only sparingly enforced by the TWQB and its Bexar County delegate agency, the understaffed San Antonio Metropolitan Health District. Actually, much of the criticism has centered around Yantis, the Executive Director. Not only is he quite political (a normal and expected orientation for directors of State boards and commissions), but it is also charged that he spends more time courting industries and developers with poor water quality records than in enforcing existing regulations. There had been a movement in Houston seeking his ouster after he was lobbying federally for several corporations which were discharging chemical wastes into the Houston ship channel in favor of the repeal of the 1899 Refuse Act which the industries were violating. Yantis has been active regularly in promoting industrial pollution positions in meetings and hearings outside of Texas, using the credibility of his public office of the state. In recognition of Yantis' nefarious activities, the Texas House Appropriations Committee voted in 1973 to halve his salary at the TWQB, because "Yantis about half does the job." With his assiduously maintained legislative alliances, however, he was restored his full salary level by the full House, losing only some dignity and respect in the affair.[26]

More importantly for SAR, Yantis was a former business associate of Hayden Head, and was convinced to take an active role in development and promotion of the project. He was one of the first public officials in Texas to learn of the SAR proposal early in 1970. He and Honts together worked on the problems that they realized SAR would provoke, both environmentally and politically. This cooperation was entirely informal, however, since no TWQB action on SAR was required by law. Yantis culminated this period of cooperation in December 1970, with a formal letter as Executive Director of the TWQB endorsing SAR as the proposal then stood. This move was designed to assure HUD that all reasonable precautions had been exercised regarding the aquifer. HUD accepted these assurances for SAR review purposes, but at the trial DeVito admitted that the TWQB was not to be relied upon for enforcement of SAR water quality safeguards.

From the start, Yantis acted as a ready advocate for SAR and its developers. When the first problems were encountered at AACOG, during the A-95 review, Yantis appeared at the GARC meeting on behalf of SAR, even though previously he had continually refused direct invitations from AACOG to attend meetings on Edwards Aquifer matters. During the November and December 1971 debates in San Antonio, Yantis made several visits to neutral and opposition groups and individuals, especially the TWQB junior associates SARA and EUWD, attempting to dissuade them from any negative resolutions. Both of those agencies had had their powers diminished by TWQB authority, but had not observed any concomitant improvement in water pollution prevention. Both agencies passed their resolutions anyway—actions which then provoked Yantis to seek and obtain an even stronger endorsement of SAR from his board (on December 16, 1971).

Yantis once again performed as front advocate for the SAR developers during the WQARB meetings that HUD and the developers organized to involve local public agencies in the technical water quality studies then being conducted. He lent himself to be chairman and benign overseer of the mostly innocuous proceedings, but was able to answer or parry sensitive questions as they were raised and conferred credibility on the whole affair. Despite the absence of formal ratification by the WQARB of the study findings, Yantis waited less than a week before presenting them to his board and receiving another unanimous formal endorsement of the SAR program, over bitter opposition of citizen groups represented at the TWQB meeting.

Prior to the SAR trial in 1973, a revealing intrigue involving Yantis and the TWQB occurred concerning the question of equal access to all available information by both sides. At the pretrial hearing the previous December, the plaintiffs were assured by the defense to the judge's satisfaction that they already had all pertinent materials on SAR from the developers, HUD, and the TWQB. Yet in January Keith Burris, the new Bexar County assistant district attorney on the case, accidentally learned of a memo prepared by the TWQB's chief geologist, Bob Hill, the previous summer, evaluating the findings of the developer water quality studies. In the memo, Hill disagreed with SAR geologist Turk's optimistic findings, concluding from the same data that storm runoff from SAR constituted a serious pollution hazard to the aquifer which probably could not be obviated. His summary prediction was that because of SAR and the adjacent development it would spawn, "within a few short years, the water supply for San Antonio would have to be treated . . . to safeguard the health of its residents."[27]

Burris eventually managed to obtain a copy of the memo, which had been suppressed by Executive Director Yantis, but it required the intervention of the Texas Attorney General John Hill (no relation) to get it. The TWQB had originally defied the attorney general in joining the SAR suit on the side of the developers. Then Yantis, as head of a public agency, refused access to a memo and its writer to Bexar County, an administrative unit of the state, while maintaining full disclosure to the private SAR developers. Subsequently, Yantis dismissed Attorney General Hill from his legal duties as trial lawyer for the TWQB, declaring that his own general counsel would try the case. Burris wrote the attorney General's office protesting Yantis' partisan actions, which elicited from Yantis a strong letter to Burris' superior, District Attorney Ted Butler, accusing Burris of unprofessional conduct in publicizing matters in the SAR case. The whole series serves to emphasize the independent and fragmented nature of government in Texas and to demonstrate the manner in which a public agency like the TWQB can serve private interests overtly and with impunity.

Both Yantis and his then chairman Fulcher were among the few persons involved in the entire SAR controversy who introduced any note of ideology into the arguments. Both were staunch defenders of private enterprise and rights of land ownership as immutable laws of society, the USA, Texas, and the TWQB. They viewed much of the opposition to SAR as part of a fundamental conflict forever raging of private rights versus public encroachment—the opposition was at-

tempting to confiscate (without just compensation) the legal development rights of the SAR site. The TWQB, as a result, defined its role
in water quality protection as one of devising the optimal standards
compatible with most private development. Any thought of forbidding
development altogether from the recharge zone was anathema. Even
zoning controls were considered by Yantis to be an unwarranted intrusion on the private sector.

In many respects the TWQB role in the SAR case was a crucial
factor in the ultimate outcome at HUD and on the local level. As the
only water quality agency actually to endorse SAR, but also as the
most relevant agency thereto, HUD could reassure itself that (1) SAR
conformed to the real necessities of the critical aquifer problem, and
(2) that the public agencies responsible for the aquifer felt the same
way. Not fully comprehending the political dynamics of this State
agency, HUD officials could be persuaded by Honts that the problems
were under control. Likewise, the TWQB became a model for convincing such recalcitrants as the San Antonio City Council that SAR
would be compelled to be implemented in such a way as to minimize
hazards to the aquifer. After all, regardless of the politics, TWQB
still was the only public agency authorized to regulate such developments.

The role of the TWQB on SAR implies certain limitations of Texas
State government in making and enforcing policy on sensitive matters.
The TWQB composition is typical of the 140 odd boards and commissions of the state. It is small, quasi-independent, and vulnerable to
politicking at the expense of the public interest. The necessity of
building and maintaining an empire tends to produce the sorts of relationships with client groups that Yantis has been involved in too
much. When challenged, the agency retreats to its best allies. Such
a situation does not bode well for innovation in policy or stringency
in regulation, which are needed in the case of water quality, and will
be needed for new communities. One cannot be optimistic about lodging
further responsibilities at the state level with public agencies which
seem to exist chiefly to serve private interests.

## THE POLITICS OF FEDERAL POLICY

### HUD Decision Making on SAR

The SAR application had never raised very much excitement among
the staff reviewers in the Office of New Communities Development in
HUD. But the project had progressed steadily if not smoothly from its

Pre-Application form of a university-centered new community, through its revised Pre-Application as a suburban satellite city with a technical center for low-skilled manpower training, to its Final Application with the same concept, submitted in November 1970. As a result of the change in midstream in the basic orientation of SAR, the project was referred to as a "retread." It was considered a mediocre new community project, and the ONCD staff was interested mostly in the truly outstanding applications.

Normally, SAR would have been killed in the review process at ONCD, but SAR was not a normal project. For one thing, Honts and his consultants were promoting SAR as the one project in the country that would benefit a Mexican-American population. The technical center would provide training for low-skill persons in conjunction with SAR industries, attracting potential workers, primarily Mexican-Americans, from the inner city of San Antonio. The proposal was not backed by any funding commitments (except $150,000 from the developers). But the minority-group focus was being actively solicited by HUD Assistant Secretary Samuel Jackson, head of the New Communities Program. Through his support, one marginal new community application, St. Charles Communities in Maryland, which contained a preponderance of low- and moderate-income housing, was approved, and another, Soul City, was being nurtured along until it too acceptably met standards for project approval. SAR was considered in the same class.

A second reason was a feeling in HUD that SAR provided a unique opportunity for proving that technology could solve environmental problems to make SAR into a model ecological community. This perceived challenged helped to raise ONCD staff enthusiasm for SAR considerably.

Finally, and most importantly, the ONCD staff review process was being conducted under an unusually strong degree of pressure from outside. Political pressure is normal and expected in federal decision making, and congressmen and other high officials had had an effect on project review before. But with its connections on both sides of the political fence, SAR was formidable politically. With George Christian, principal in the CMH firm, a press secretary to former President Johnson, and a close associate of then Treasury Secretary Connally, SAR had a potent direct link to high Administration circles. Although he denied it, Connally was believed to have an investment interest in SAR also, either directly or through one of his investment corporations such as had speculated in land near the UTSA site. In addition, with Hayden Head (along with Lawrence Wood) as an influential Texas Republican, and a friend of Senator Tower, the SAR team had another line of influence to the Administration political circles.

Texas was considered a high-priority area, for both votes and campaign funds, by the Nixon reelection strategists during 1970 and 1971. The White House administrators, through whom all major federal project approvals had to pass, were at the time looking quite favorably on projects that by strategic associations and locations would enhance the president's reelection efforts. New communities were viewed in this category—as high-visibility, large-scale federal commitments which, while fulfilling their objectives, could be politically beneficial. As a result, Texas had more new communities either fully or tentatively approved by HUD prior to the 1972 election than any other state.

The benevolent White House eyes on Texas, plus the considerable supplications through Connally and Tower, placed SAR's staff review in a different light. The White House let it be known to its political officials in HUD that SAR was a top priority. This was the more or less regular interference in the new communities project review process which ONCD Director William Nicoson denounced at the time of his resignation in May 1972. He claimed that the New Communities Program was not viable as long as political decisions and appropriations freezes were Administration policy. HUD Secretary George Romney echoed these sentiments in his resignation speech in November 1972, but broadened them to blame partisan politics for the inability of HUD to address urban problems.

Whether or not the White House support of SAR was tied to the agreement of Christian, Connally, and Head to work actively for Nixon's 1972 campaign is not known. It is likely that some quid pro quo was involved, especially for Christian, defecting from his Democratic Party but without the statesmanlike image or Republican ambitions then possessed by Connally. An analogous bargain was apparently struck on the HUD guaranteed new community of Soul City in North Carolina. This project, sponsored by former CORE director Floyd McKissick, was weak in terms of feasibility and unlikely to obtain a loan guarantee commitment, until an agreement was reached between McKissick and the White House, through black aide Robert J. Brown, for McKissick to become a Republican and to campaign for Nixon. After that, the ONCD staff worked diligently with McKissick's staff, revising and improving the Soul City application to bring it to acceptable standards for project approval.[28]

The SAR Final Application was similarly reworked and amended over a long period of time, culminating just prior to the explosion of the issue in San Antonio in October 1971. The ONCD staff claims that no new community receives approval that does not meet rigorous criteria—no bad project is ever guaranteed. But many new community applications represent good projects, and through revision some had projects can be made acceptable. The applications with the greatest political muscle behind them can thus attain top priority status.

Sometime prior to the submittal of ONCD staff recommendations on a new community project to the CDC board, the review takes on a momentum of its own, regardless of the politics involved. This condition is true of many bureaucratic project reviews. In a way, however, the ONCD review process itself reinforces this point of no return, since it is designed from the first contact with a developer to weed out infeasible projects through a system of progressive check points. Thus when a new community proposal reaches the stage of submittal of a Final Application, representing a half million dollars or so investment on the part of the developer, the ONCD staff itself is quite committed to a favorable recommendation on the project and will do what is necessary to overcome obstacles thereto.

For SAR, such obstacles were many. One of the first of these was the environmental impact statement, to be prepared prior to the completion of favorable staff review, before submitting a project to the CDC for final approval, under the NEPA of 1969. For every major project action, all federal agencies are required to prepare and circulate to the Council on Environmental Quality (CEQ) and other pertinent agencies an EIS discussing

1. the environmental impact of the proposed action
2. any adverse environmental effects which cannot be avoided should the project be implemented
3. alternatives to the proposed action
4. the relationship between local short-term uses of man's environment and the maintenance and enhancement of long-term productivity
5. any irreversible and irretrievable commitments of resources which would be involved in the proposed action should it be implemented. [29]

All new communities under the Title VII program have been interpreted to be major federal project actions. But Title VII is unusual since the project initiative emanates from a private developer, not a federal agency. In practice, therefore, the EIS for Title VII new communities has become an odious additional task that HUD delegates to the developer after tentative project approval but before formal ratification by the CDC. According to the intent of NEPA, HUD is responsible for, and rightly should prepare, the EIS, but the developer has most of the information and the ONCD staff is very limited. Although the developer primarily prepares the EIS for the ONCD staff, the effort is made cooperative through the participation of the Community and

Environmental Standards Office (CESO) and the review of the Environmental Clearance Section of the General Counsel's Office, both of which oversee all HUD statements.

When the SAR Draft EIS was being readied for publication in September 1971, HUD officials apparently were aware of the potential in it for exploitation by concerned environmentalists. The hazards SAR could pose for the aquifer were acknowledged, but such sections as alternatives to the action and irreversible resource commitments did not fit the Title VII new community program well, due to the private-public duality. The Draft EIS therefore glossed over the required environmental appraisals with respect to the real hazards of SAR. Everybody concerned—the developer, the ONCD staff, the CESO staff, and the General Counsel staff monitoring it—all seemed to be aware of the flaws in the EIS. But pressures from Assistant Secretary Jackson's office were constant and succeeded in squelching any over-zealous review of the Draft EIS, in HUD Washington, in HUD Region VI in Fort Worth, and even in the CEQ.

The Draft EIS triggered a second major obstacle for the HUD staff to overcome—the vehement opposition to SAR in San Antonio. The commitment of the ONCD (and Jackson) to SAR was evident in the time and effort expended in explaining and defending SAR in the local area. Never, it seems, was there any thought given to abandonment of the project, or even of postponing its submittal to the CDC, although lack of local approval would have cast an ominous shadow on SAR and HUD. Ironically, just as HUD was deepest in its commitment to SAR, the developers were debating selling out to the "butchers." The pressures and promises from HUD on SAR did finally succeed in turning City Council sentiment around, and the staff could proceed with its Final EIS and its recommendation to the CDC.

The five-member CDC is composed of political appointees who are charged with final responsibility in the approval of Title VII loan guarantee commitments. At the time of the SAR approval, the chairman was Secretary Romney, and the other members were James M. Beggs, Undersecretary of the Department of Transportation, HUD Assistant Secretary Floyd M. Hyde, New York financial consultant John G. Heimann, and HUD Assistant Secretary Jackson, the General Manager of the CDC. All were politically sensitive enough to have been touched by the pressures for early approval of SAR. The board acceded readily to the ONCD staff recommendation, including the unique "commitment with conditions," a rider never before attached to an offer of commitment which required environmental studies to be made on SAR prior to final loan guarantee certification. Approval with such significant conditions indicated a pent-up haste to move SAR ahead and to remove the insistent pressures pushing for acceptance. The ONCD staff could be relieved, too, since 1971 had been such an horrendous year for Title VII (only two guarantees out of a scheduled ten) that maybe 1972 could now proceed apace.

One other problem that plagued the ONCD during the SAR review was an obstinate refusal to play dead by the HUD Region VI Office in Fort Worth. Despite the decentralization that HUD had been undergoing into regional and area offices, the New Communities Program remained concentrated at headquarters in Washington. Except for the EIS process, the ONCD did not even make a pretense of involving the regional and area offices in new community applications. There were no staff assignments at either level with any significant function concerning new communities in their territories. This situation was perfect for the SAR developers, whose best line of political communication was directly to Washington.

But Richard Morgan, HUD Administrator for Region VI in Fort Worth, was convinced that large-scale HUD commitments like Title VII new communities, with their priority and supplementary grants for infrastructure, should not be allowed to bypass the regional offices, despite the difficulty in finding or assigning specialized personnel for this purpose to all offices. As a political appointee himself, Morgan had certain channels open to him and utilized them to lobby for inclusion of new communities within the purview of his regional office. Since the case in point at this time was SAR, Morgan thus provided another headache for ONCD staff in their attempts to smooth out the SAR problems. It has been speculated that Morgan also had a role in sending the go/no-go letter with the Draft EIS to Planning Director Davis in October 1971 which initiated the local conflict. In any event, Morgan gradually won concessions from Washington, beginning with carbon copies. Other concessions followed, including a full-time staff member (New Communities Liaison Officer) and some operational monitoring responsibilities for new communities projects once development is underway.

Federal Impact on Local Areas

The politics of SAR and HUD's attempt to implement a new community there can also be seen as manifestations of a larger movement toward greater federal determination of local policy, and therefore as inevitable. It could be argued that the uniform and massive federal programs since World War II are more responsible than any other single element for the urban landscape today. FHA home mortgage insurance, interstate highways, and urban renewal have changed the face of American cities in less than 30 years. New communities are but a new addition to this group. But, more importantly, the increasing scarcity of local financial resources and availability of federal categorical funds over the years more and more limited the effective range of policy choices open to local governments. They found themselves in a "take-it-or-leave-it" position regarding federal funds, which were vital to their existence but carried rigid guidelines for utilization.

> Most administrators expressed the opinion that federal programs themselves, by the way they are structured and funded, determine to a great extent activities to be undertaken by the city, and therefore influence priorities. "The federal government calls the tune by the programs it funds," one official stated.[30]

Federal administration has made use of what are known as "carrots and sticks" to encourage and to force compliance with federal policy already made. Local governments' scope for the exercise of discretion in policy making thus tended to become smaller.

In the case of SAR, carrots and sticks were in evidence quite often. First of all, the SAR plans themselves were altered at HUD's request to bring the project more into accord with Title VII regulations, which themselves had been written to conform to the standard model of new community success—Columbia, Maryland—from the developer of which much of the ONCD staff originated.[31] HUD was actually attempting to encourage the development of new communities across the nation which would uniformly resemble a single model in physical, social, economic, and governmental structure. In this attempt, a developer making application to HUD had little choice available, and the community in which the project was to be located had even less.

Secondly, when the conflict on SAR began in earnest on the local level, HUD held out the possibility of a new town in-town being approved in addition to SAR, as well as all the normal housing, redevelopment, and community facilities funding. HUD even asked the SAR developers to investigate the feasibility of developing a new town in-town to alleviate the heated attention on SAR by dangling another "goody" in front of local eyes. San Antonio was being informed, in effect, that if it endorsed SAR it could be in line for an additional major federal project.

A final example of carrots and sticks on SAR was the blatant strategy employed by the SAR developers during November and December 1971 of threatening a cutoff of HUD funds to San Antonio if SAR were not approved. A complete freeze on such funds was of course absurd, but an unofficial use of administrative stalling and equivocating was (and is) common enough to act as a real threat to anyone concerned with federally funded programs (which is to say practically all public officials).

In effect, San Antonio—and in particular the City Council—was operating within a very narrow range of alternatives. It could approve SAR and expect a continuation of existing federal support, plus (or minus) whatever effects SAR might bring, or it could reject SAR and jeopardize any future new community application, as well as other project funding. A real impact of HUD policy on SAR, then, was on local politics in San Antonio in biasing the scope of the politics, both as the process by which community values are expressed and as the allocation of community resources.

Viewed from another perspective, however,

> It may be argued persuasively that the national government is more sensitive to public needs in the beginning and more subject to popular control in the end than are either state or local governments. . . . On the one hand, "centralization" turns out on examination to be more a war cry of embattled local interests than a trend; but on the other hand true centralization, if it should come to exist, would represent a trend in power and influence from generally less democratic governments toward a generally more democratic government, from bewildered state and local governments toward a government with some sense of national urgency and mission.[32]

This argument can point to federal activities in civil rights, education, antipoverty, and other areas in which federal initiative was essential before any action would occur on the state and local levels. In such instances, local policy determination was not adequate to meet national policy objectives, and the federal actions had to override local reactions.

In a large sense, the above presents a dilemma of whether national policy (such as Title VII) as conceived and implemented should uniformly take precedence over local policy decisions differentially established in the local political arena. As noted in the SAR experience, private interests affect policy and administration in both places, and there are no guidelines by which to assess the merits of any given policy. To minimize conflict in implementing policy at odds with local situations, the federal government has increasingly used carrots and sticks as more "subtle" strategy for obtaining compliance with its policy, rather than any form of direct intervention. Under this technique, state and local governments are given incentives to comply or penalties for noncompliance, which then biases their own policy making but nevertheless leaves the ultimate decisions in their hands.

But along with the growth in the ability of the federal government to narrow the range of policy options for local areas, a relatively new phenomenon has emerged to challenge federal actions from the grass roots. Citizen groups, acting as "private attorneys general," have increasingly utilized their recourse to legal channels to obtain strict adherence of federal agencies to proper procedures and consistent substance in their project decisions. Manifested particularly with respect to the environment (under NEPA and other legislation), this now firmly established power of private citizens to question federal policy has tended to restore some of the balance to federal-local relations. Germinating unexpectedly at a time of maximum federal domination of local decisions, this citizen power has been frightening to federal bureaucracies in its basically unorganized and irrational striking at the implementation of projects which are the easiest to block or with the most at stake. Although theoretically such legal action seeks compliance with existing federal legislation, it is basically negative and lacking in any policy foundation. This countervailing force, as disruptive and undemocratic as it may be, has been part of a new type of politics based on conflict through which a different equilibrium in federal-local relations may be evolving.

At much the same time, federal policy with regard to local governments has been changing, with the introduction of the "New Federalism" programs of revenue sharing and community development block grants as vehicles of federal assistance. These approaches represent a strategic retreat by the federal government from its unopposed advances of the 1960s into determining local policy choices. This reversal implies a lessening both of the federal carrots-and-sticks tactical impact and federal initiatives so important to social change in the last decade. The emerging style fosters greater discretion at the local governmental level, where policy is least consistent and where conflict is on the rise. More unallocated federal assistance also leads to more constituencies battling for their shares of the pot. In general, however, the new freedom of choices available to local governments will not greatly affect the federal impact on local areas, since lacking the spirit of innovation, most unencumbered funds will probably be spent on the same type projects the federal government encouraged to be undertaken through the years. Taken together with the rising power of citizen groups, the new federal assistance policy suggests a high level of conflict as the characterization of the future federal-local relationship—a legacy of federal domination, and probably an unstable one until the advent of new federal initiatives.

In many ways, then, the SAR experience had one foot in the old and one in the new. SAR was the product of a federal program policy output manifested on the local level, which neither the state nor the local governments could have or would have conceived or implemented on their own. Carrots and sticks were utilized by HUD (in league with the developer) to obtain compliance with its policy, were resented by the locals, but were victorious in the end by exploiting natural cleavages in the local politics. But the level of conflict aroused in the process, followed by the lengthy citizen legal opposition, nearly managed to sink the project permanently, presaging new types of relationships in the future between federal policy and local impact.

The application of this emerging political model to the future of new communities in general is analyzed in Chapter 4.

NOTES

1. See A Report on Population: San Antonio and Bexar County (San Antonio: Comprehensive Planning Division, Community Development Office, City of San Antonio, May, 1973), p. 55.

2. Oliver P. Williams and Charles R. Adrian, Four Cities: A Study in Comparative Policy Making (Philadelphia: University of Pennsylvania Press, 1963), p. 23.

3. J. David Greenstone and Paul E. Peterson, "Reformers, Machines, and the War on Poverty," in James Q. Wilson, ed., City Politics and Public Policy (New York: John Wiley & Sons, Inc., 1968), pp. 269-71.

4. Robert L. Lineberry and Edmund P. Fowler, "Reformism and Public Policies in American Cities," in Wilson, op. cit., p. 122.

5. William Crane, "Government and Politics in San Antonio," in Leonard E. Goodall, ed., Urban Politics in the Southwest (Tempe, Ariz.: Institute of Public Administration, Arizona State University, 1967), p. 135.

6. Edwin M. Epstein, The Corporation in American Politics (Englewood Cliffs, N.J.: Prentice-Hall, Inc., 1969), p. 237.

7. Robert R. Alford, Bureaucracy and Participation (Chicago: Rand McNally & Co., 1969), p. 194.

8. Robert E. Agger, Daniel Goldrich, and Bert E. Swanson, The Rulers and the Ruled (New York: John Wiley & Sons, Inc., 1964), p. 19.

9. See The Texas Observer, September 30, 1966, and January 10, 1969.

10. Peter Bachrach and Morton S. Baratz, Power and Poverty: Theory and Practice (New York: Oxford University Press, 1970), pp. 47-48.

11. Murray S. Stedman, Jr., Urban Politics (Cambridge, Mass.: Winthrop Publishers, 1972), p. 233.

12. E. E. Schattschneider, The Semi-Sovereign People (New York: Holt, Rinehart and Winston, Inc., 1960), p. 71.

13. Raymond E. Wolfinger, "Nondecisions and the Study of Local Politics," American Political Science Review, Vol. 65, No. 4 (December 1971), p. 1072.

14. Richard M. Merelman, "On the Neo-Elitist Critique of Community Power," American Political Science Review, Vol. 62, No. 2 (June 1968), p. 456.

15. See Wolfinger, op. cit., p. 1071.

16. Stedman, op. cit., p. 12.

17. San Antonio Express, June 17, 1973.

18. Merelman, op. cit., p. 454.

19. Nelson W. Polsby, Community Power and Political Theory (New Haven: Yale University Press, 1963), pp. 8-11.

20. Crane, op. cit., p. 139.

21. See Office of Management and Budget, Circular A-95 (July 24, 1969); revised (February 9, 1971); revised (November 13, 1973).

22. Clifton McClesky, The Government and Politics of Texas, 3rd ed. (Boston: Little, Brown and Co., 1969), pp. 202-04.

23. Texas Water Code, Title 2, Chap. 21, Sec. 21.002.

24. Ibid., Sec. 21.022.

25. Texas Water Quality Board Order No. 70-0731-12.

26. San Antonio Express, March 30, 1973.

27. Bob Hill, TWQB Inter-Office Memorandum: "Comments on the Special Report by L. J. Turk to the San Antonio Ranch Water Quality Advisory Review Board Dated May 11, 1972," June 1, 1972.

28. See Newsweek, August 14, 1972, p. 23.

29. National Environmental Policy Act of 1969, P. L. 91-190, Sec. 102(2)(C); 42 U.S.C. 4331 (2)(C).

30. Oakland Task Force, San Francisco Federal Executive Board, Federal Decision Making and Impact in Urban Areas: A Study of Oakland (New York: Praeger Publishers, 1970), p. 48.

31. Robert Tennenbaum, "New Communities in the Seventies, Part I: St. Charles Communities, Maryland, and Flower Mound, Texas," in Shirley F. Weiss, Edward J. Kaiser, and Raymond J. Burby III, eds., New Community Development: Planning Process, Implementation, and Emerging Social Concerns, Vol. 1 (Chapel Hill, N. C.: New Towns Research Seminar, Center for Urban and Regional Studies, University of North Carolina at Chapel Hill, 1971), p. 443.

32. Roscoe C. Martin, The Cities and the Federal System (New York: Atherton Press, 1965), pp. 191-92.

# 4

## NEW COMMUNITIES
## AND THE
## PUBLIC INTEREST

The critique of San Antonio Ranch as a political issue provided certain insights into the patterns of local politics and the dynamics of federal-local relations, but it did not address the significance of SAR for the future of governmentally sponsored new communities. The central question becomes one of how can such new communities be made more responsive to the concept of the "public interest?" New communities are a genre of relatively recent origin which has inherent normative overtones of improving the quality of community life. In recent years the development of new communities has been a burgeoning enterprise, but with relatively few precedents on which to rely. Yet by its very nature its consequences have great impact on the lives of many people—effects until recently left largely undefined and uncontrolled. With the entrance of the federal government into new communities as a development partner, a greater sense of responsibility for protecting and enhancing the public interests involved has been gradually emerging.

The following sections will examine the SAR experience for its implications for the developer and governmental roles in Title VII new communities, and will present a few proposals for more effective and responsible new community development. Once again the analysis and conclusions are based on the SAR case, as well as pertinent literature related thereto.

## IMPLICATIONS OF SAR FOR NEW COMMUNITIES

### The Developer Role

For a developer there are a great many differences between conventional new communities and the more recent Title VII (and formerly
Title IV) new communities. The basic difference is of course that the
developer has a major partner in his entrepreneurship—the federal
government. But this condition can be both an advantage and a dis-
advantage, a benefit and a cost. On the plus side, the loan guarantees
and the supplementary grants make projects more feasible economically than they would have been otherwise, due to the difficulties in
obtaining financing for large developments and the enormous early
project costs. In addition, the federal participation enables and encourages developers to broaden the range of amenities, institutions,
and functions in the new communities over what the conventional conservative development approach normally produced.

On the other hand, however, the time delays, the uncertainties,
the additional plan requirements, the extra documentation, and the
substantial fees that accompany the Title VII process can be enough
to destroy the delicate balance of cash flow and timing that have always
been the mainstays of real estate development. One noted developer
expressed these sentiments:

> There is quite a paradox in the whole Title IV operation
> which is quite a challenge to the developer. The paradox
> is that the intent of Title IV is to encourage the develop-
> ment of new communities. It says so right in the Act. But,
> when you get into the philosophy and the nitty-gritty of the
> administration of it, you begin to wonder. There is no
> question in my mind that to do a new town under Title IV
> is to do it the hard way. . . . It requires an incredible act
> of faith on the part of the developer, particularly experi-
> enced developers, to get involved in Title IV. The com-
> plexities of getting decisions made on time and of coordi-
> nating all of the various inputs that have to be coordinated
> to get that next thing done is something you cannot imagine
> unless you have lived through it. [1]

Developers nevertheless flocked to Title IV and Title VII with their
proposals and applications, at least for the first few years, thus
tending to confirm that the advantages outweighed the disadvantages
in most cases. Even the developer quoted above subsequently applied

for and received approval of Title VII loan guarantees for a new community project of his. However, the type of developer attracted to the program was not primarily the experienced land developer or homebuilder. The predominant type was from other sectors of activity, usually with real estate investments and interested primarily in the profits or power to be derived from new community development (as with SAR, where it was Head and CMH, not the large local developers, who came forward with the new community proposal). This inexperience, coupled with the devastating effect of the 1974 recession on most real estate developments, is widely blamed for many Title VII new community difficulties. Conversely, the economic conditions, together with the ever-increasing requirements, documentation, and controls that evolved as the HUD response to New Communities Program problems, had by 1974 reduced developer interest in Title VII virtually to nil.

Because of the partnership involved in Title VII, those new Communities developed under its authority are, on the whole, different from conventional new communities.[2] There is no standard or model conventional (non-Title VII) new community; they are quite diverse. But most that have been developed to date are primarily aimed at the middle- and upper-income groups (and retirees) and are essentially satellite bedroom communities, differing from other suburbs only in the single ownership, multiple land uses, and general plan. The Title VII legislation is specific in stating that a new community is eligible under its authority only if it

1. will provide an alternative to disorderly urban growth, helping preserve or enhance desirable aspects of the natural and urban environment . . .

2. will be economically feasible in terms of economic base or potential for economic growth

3. will contribute to the welfare of the entire area which will be substantially affected by the program and of which the land to be developed is a part

4. is consistent with comprehensive planning, physical and social . . . (including state, local, and private plans) . . .

5. has received all governmental reviews and approvals required by State or local law, or by the Secretary

6. will contribute to good living conditions in the community . . . will be characterized by well-balanced and diversified land use patterns and will include or be served by adequate public, community, and commercial facilities . . .

7. makes substantial provision for housing within the means of persons of low and moderate income . . .

8. will make significant use of advances in design and technology. . . .[3]

Although the Title VII legislation mandates a different and better kind of new community than the real estate market was previously producing, the implementation process for Title VII has failed to evolve with a distinctly innovative identity. The extra documentation and delays of the Title VII review process do enable HUD ultimately to determine any or all of the particulars of an approved new community. Since the resulting new community product is as much HUD's as the developer's, the new community as presented to the state and local levels of government and the citizenry of the area is a hybrid of real estate development and major federal project action. A Title VII new community project, such as SAR, is reviewed on the state and local levels, therefore, as if it were a conventional real estate development and a federal action—separately, disjointedly, and somewhat irrationally. This situation is due partly to the unusual partnership created by Title VII, and partly to the newness of the program itself. But the lack of a distinctly different process of implementation and review, to account for the unique properties and impacts of the Title VII program, has led to the sorts of problems recounted above for SAR.

The dichotomous nature of Title VII governmental relations and review has evolved because the two partners—the developer and the federal government—have entirely different interests at stake in the new community vis-a-vis state and local governments. The developer has very specific needs:

> The three most critical desires of the developer are that he be aided financially, that he be left alone by government and regulation as much as possible, and that the integrity of the plan will be protected by government procedures so that the developer's concepts will be reflected in the completed development. If the developer is too restricted, the development may never occur. If he is left to control his own actions, the state may find itself with some severe problems. . . . [4]

The federal government, under Title VII, has come to the aid of the developer in the first and the third wishes at the expense of the second. In return, the developer is required to comply with the many criteria formulated describing what a new community should be like.

What is still missing is any comprehensive involvement of state and local governmental entities. The developer, although accustomed to operating at the local level, feels less obligated under Title VII to make his case for the new community in the local area because the Feds have assumed responsibility for the project, and the HUD regulations are specific only in demanding the securing of "all state and local reviews and approvals required by law" and "the adoption by the local governing body of a resolution . . . approving the new community program."[5] The principal review a developer must undergo during the application phase then is the A-95 process through the local clearinghouse (in the case of SAR—AACOG), because it is a federal project. A developer may interpret this required review as the only necessary interaction with the local governmental agencies.

Most developers remain cynical regarding local reviews because their experience in conventional real estate development (and/or other) governmental relations has been less than satisfactory:

> Every time you go down to the county planning commission or the county board of supervisors for the approval of a subdivision or for a zoning appeal, there will be a group of noisy uninformed amateur planners . . . there to shoot you down. And, the planning commission and the county commissioners with their ear to the next election are going to listen to them.[6]

Developers are even a little paranoid about new communities and the local citizenry:

> You've got a very tricky proposition in making a presentation to public bodies and to staff people if you are in an area where nothing particularly outstanding has been developed. The problem comes about because they are all living in the way you say you are going to improve. You cannot put the typical subdivision on this wall and your own magnificent plan on that wall and expect any cheers. They live in the typical subdivision. So, it's difficult. You say that there will be culture and this and that and he says, what's in it for me?[7]

Under Title VII, the new community developer is both better and worse off in these governmental relations. He is in a worse position because he is forced by regulations to seek certain approvals and carry on certain public relations in an overt and straightforward manner. He is, however, in a more favorable light since he is marketing a product that has the considerable weight and credibility of the federal government behind it. For SAR, this identification helped immensely, in the assistance that HUD (once fully committed to SAR) provided the developer in local meetings and in the devious promises and threats dispensed by the developers in their efforts to influence key decision makers.

During the AACOG A-95 review process for SAR, the developers were going through a full governmental relations stage—a necessity for being a major federal project as well as a new community. Later on, it was the additional burden of being a federal project that conferred vulnerability on SAR (that is, the EIS) and reopened the public review. When the developers first began the counteroffensive, the tactics utilized were more akin to those of real estate operators in local politics than the defense of a proposed federal project. In other words, with backs to the wall the Title VII developers reverted to political instincts associated with conventional new community projects and their builders. Finally, when the political battle in San Antonio was won and the legal action initiated, the SAR posture was once again that of defending a federally sponsored project from environmentalist vigilantes. The course of the SAR experience demonstrates clearly the dichotomous and disjointed nature of Title VII governmental relations.

New community developers are becoming more sophisticated in their implementation strategies as more new communities are constructed and studied and as more developers grasp the enormous potential for profit and power in new communities. Traditionally,

> most of the community builders have been relatively unaware of the long-term importance of local government and of the near-irreversible nature of many local decisions made early in the development process. Moreover, the developers have concentrated on (1) their financial position during the early years, and (2) the problems of physical planning for their communities. [8]

Now, however, developers are moving more toward planning for governmental relations, and even planning for opposition. Although much of the SAR history was punctuated by a reluctance of the developers even to approach local governments, once they were forcibly embroiled in local politics a certain sophistication in planning strategy was unmistakable. It is little wonder that more effective tactics would be employed by a team of self-proclaimed "politicians" rather than traditional community developers mired in customary real estate politics. Such tactics also alienated, at least temporarily, some of the more traditionalist local developers.

The SAR case history suggests a couple of recent theoretical approaches to project implementation. Bodnar and Wassenich have focused on key stages of new community development. The second, the "control" stage, concerns governmental relations. Groups of actors can be categorized as "gainers" or "losers," reflecting their

TABLE 2

Gainers and Losers in Land Development

| Actors | Perceived Short-run | Actual Short-run | Perceived Long-run | Actual Long-run |
|---|---|---|---|---|
| Speculators near planned community | G | G | G | G |
| Private utility owners | G | G | G | G |
| Construction unions | G | G | L–G | G |
| Local businessmen | G | G | G | L |
| Political "outs" | G | L–G | G | L–G |
| The very poor | L | G | L–G | G |
| The displaced | L | G | G | L |
| Local planners | L | L–G | L | G |
| Successful farmers | L | G | L | L |
| Landowner-dwellers near planned community | L | L | L | G |
| Local bureaucrats | L | L | L | G |
| Other developers | L | L | L | L–G |
| Local politicians in power | L | L–G | L | L |

L=losers                                                   G=gainers

potentials for being affected by the development of a new community. The accompanying table illustrates the concept. Bodnar and Wassenich point out that a developer should seek out those actors who perceive short-run gains and those actors who have actual short-run gains, the latter needing their gains made explicit to them. Those who perceive short-run losses should be considered the greatest direct obstacles. [9]

Then there are courses of action by which the obstacle actors can be overcome through the utilization of developer resources. Examples of the courses of action, ranging from lowest to highest consumption of resources, are (1) ignore them; (2) dilute them; (3) subvert them; (4) coalite them; and (5) overwhelm them. [10] Since political, as well as financial, resources available to a developer are limited, the rational developer seeks to pass through the delicate "control," or governmental relations, stage of implementation as low down the continuum as possible, in order to minimize resource outlays. If the terminology for the courses of action rings of military strategy, it serves to underscore the seriousness and cynicism with which politics is perceived and played. Planning for political action can only be more so.

Another approach to project implementation is developed in Wolpert's series on conflict in public facility locational decisions. The thrust of the work is that in planning for large-scale projects (for example, expressways and new communities) the traditional cost-minimization models are inadequate in not accounting for such important effects as potential delays caused by citizen opposition and other implementation problems that might increase costs. One of the proposed alternative approaches, the "political placation model," includes analysis of potential opposition groups and the likely impact of each one; some can be safely ignored while others require concessions or side payments to reduce their opposition. All such costs and delays are then built into the economic model as costs of development. [11]

Wolpert's models are a sophisticated but logical extension of the Bodnar and Wassenich research, and both are technically related to the SAR case. The SAR developers did not plan for the opposition, nor did they include the costs of delays into their cash-flow projections. Their political action against obstacle actors and opposition groups came late, was planned hurriedly, and was carried out on a somewhat ad hoc basis. However, the characteristics have similarities. The analysis of the opposition as of November 1971 and the campaign to overcome it were based on an analysis of who composed each opposition element, how much clout it had, what its pressure points or "price" were, how much of the developer resources should be committed to neutralizing the opposition, and how best to seek access to each element. In a similar manner, SAR allies were mobilized that had "perceived short-run gains" from the project.

In terms of actual concessions to placate opposition groups, the SAR developers had mixed success. The contract and the water quality studies were enough to overcome the City Council opposition, but not that of Bexar County and the environmental groups. Whether the developers could have arrived at a level of concessions to placate these groups is not known. In any event, their original cash-flow model was decimated by the delays and the additional costs of the concessions; perhaps it would not stretch any further without endangering economic feasibility of the entire project, even with the Title VII guarantee. Ultimately, the costs of not placating all the opposition may be the highest of all, in view of the extraordinary costs and delay of the litigation.

The implications for developers of new communities under Title VII, as well as for HUD, are many. In identifying and analyzing the probable opposition to a proposed new community, planning will have to go beyond physical, economic, social, and environmental to encompass the political. Local opposition to new communities is growing rapidly all over the country—for example, Cedar-Riverside in Minneapolis is being sued by local citizens, New Franconia in Fairfax County, Virginia, was stopped by negative local reactions, and the Rouse Company dropped two promising new community projects due to citizen opposition. And the means to delay many projects (perhaps to death) is readily available to citizen groups and local governments through legal administrative harassment. Political planning will introduce a cynical cast to the enlightened and hopeful field of new community planning, but developers will view such realistic analysis as the only choice in a business increasingly tormented by local activists, ideologues, and do-gooders.

HUD, too, can utilize the SAR experience and the political action models to view Title VII new communities as locational decisions, which have benefits and costs for any of several alternative sites. Actually, Wolpert's models are best suited to evaluation of alternative sites. New communities, especially Title VII, however, have never been conceived in terms of alternative sites, because of private developer initiative and control. It was on this account that the NEPA alternatives argument against SAR was effectively killed during the trial. But opposition is increasing in strength and ability to block or to delay new community implementation on vulnerable sites. For HUD to commit the time and resources to a prospective Title VII new community, such as SAR, and to have the project stymied once beyond the point of no return, would be a minor disaster and could have major repercussions in future policy. HUD needs to construe Title VII as a process of locational decision making like other federal project actions, and then to include costs of opposition as an integral part of its own feasibility analysis. For Title VII new communities, locational analysis would add another dimension to the HUD review of proposed projects—the merits of an application plus a benefit-cost ratio of the location, in terms of physical criteria as well as potential opposition. Such a process could also encourage cooperation with local, regional, or state governments in identifying and evaluating locations.

### The Governmental Role

There are many interests involved in any new community project, some articulated and active in the dynamics of implementation, others mostly latent and passive. A partial listing of these interests would include the following: (1) the developer's interest in making a success of his project as an investment and as a business enterprise; (2) if

Title VII, HUD's interest in carrying out the objectives of the New Communities Program in the name of the public; (3) the interests of future residents of the new community; (4) those of residents of the areas adjacent to the new community; (5) those of citizens of the city or county within which the new community is located; (6) those of the entire metropolitan area or region; and (7) the wider interest of society in the character of future urban growth and new communities, statewide and nationally. [12]

It is the role of governments to reconcile such disparate interests into some workable conception of "the public interest."[13] As the Title VII New Communities Program operates currently, HUD is the national coordinator and responsible agent for the public interest vis-a-vis the developer's interests. As the SAR events demonstrated, however, HUD cannot necessarily be relied upon even to comprehend the peculiarities and nuances of local area problems and needs, much less to act as guardian of these local public interests. On the contrary, HUD was actively in cooperation with the SAR developer to change local opinion, under the tacit assumption that the local San Antonio opposition was misguided and unintended.

It must be observed, however, that in conventional new community projects, where HUD is not a partner, the interests of most of the above-named groups are ignored or circumvented to an even greater degree than under HUD's benefaction. The abuses of "the public interest" in conventional new communities stagger the imagination, as reflected in one professional's lament:

What is really shocking is that we allow one man or one company to make such important decisions affecting the future of the community. Nobody should have the right to build a city of 50,000 or more without some effective public control of where the city is located and of everything else about it. [14]

Perhaps it could be paraphrased for Title VII new communities that such decisions are too important to be left to the developer and HUD bureaucrats in Washington.

One may ask, given the fragmented and bureaucratic nature of multilevel governmental structure, whether any government can indeed define and represent effectively all of "the public interest." Title VII new community development constitutes a unique subset of the overall problem. As a federal program, enacted by Congress presumably in the best interests of society as a whole, the question becomes one of the extent to which the New Communities Program can represent the totality of the enumerated public interests, or the responsiveness of the federal government administration to local needs and concerns. In short, we are not attempting here to debate the merits of the Title VII program as an approach to new community development in the United States; on the contrary, this work assumes throughout that the objectives and framework of the program are valid and constructive. Our aim is to evaluate the ability of the program and its administrators to represent the very real public interests in various localities throughout the United States.

Of the eight interests listed at the beginning of this section, HUD has been most successful as an advocate for itself, society nationally (as represented by the Act), and its developers. Title VII is a developer-oriented program, because of the organization as a partnership between HUD and developers. Once it has been determined that a particular new community is satisfactory to HUD, then HUD becomes the defender and protector of that new community and its developer against any threat to its successful implementation. Such is the case even when the decision to approve the new community application was made in response to political manipulation between developer and Administration, which has predetermined the HUD evaluation of the degree to which the new community met the criteria of the Act and its regulations. The HUD (and ONCD) staffs have strong needs as bureaucracies to court political favor in the search for appropriations, tenure, and long-term achievement. Simultaneously, they can act obsequiously to sources of political strength and arrogantly to their client groups at the local levels. With or without political linkages on any given project, the bureaucratic expertise and knowledgeability can lead to insularity and inertia with respect to project implementation. [15] Glimpses of such bureaucratic behavior on the part of HUD became visible in the case of SAR once a favorable decision was inevitable, regardless of the political dealings that assisted the decision.

But so far as representing the other interests is concerned, such as those of future residents and neighboring local and regional citizens, the Title VII program is improperly constituted. As a federal program, the initiative must originate at the federal level. But the SAR experience tends to shed doubts on the ability or commitment of HUD to do so effectively, at least currently. As a politically potent new community, SAR by all indications politely soft-pedaled the spirit if not the letter of the criteria relating to local citizen interests during its application review process. Once the decision had been made internally to approve SAR, HUD's interests became one with the developer's. When local opposition arose, HUD and the SAR developers staged a coordinated assault through local politics to silence it. In doing so, HUD provided the support [rebutting or denying each opposition argument and charge, and feeding suggestions, (for example, on the new town in-town) and officials to assist], while the developer carried out the visible politicking. Concessions were granted, such as the water quality review board and a conditional offer of commitment, but only with the intention of buying off the opposition. HUD could do all of this because it was confident in its ability to determine what was really in the public interest, even if the public refused to believe its interpretation.

SAR is not the only Title VII new community in which such attitudes and actions have been evident. The second new community to receive a commitment for a loan guarantee (actually under Title IV), St. Charles Communities in southeastern Maryland, was approved quickly with political pressure after obtaining pro forma endorsements from the county government. The county officials and citizens did not understand what the new community was all about, but when they learned, bitter opposition developed. The county had not at that point granted the necessary zoning, and adamantly refused to do so, buttressed by support from the state, including even the governor. Although the issues involved the plan's 80 percent low and moderate income housing, lack of employment commitments, fiscal impact disparities, and highway congestion, the case is similar to SAR in HUD's unilateral vision of the public interest surrounding a new community and the coincidence of HUD's and the developer's interests.[16]

Another analogous case is that of Soul City in North Carolina, guaranteed in June 1972. Ever since developer Floyd McKissick agreed to support former President Nixon's reelection, Soul City had received high priority in HUD to make the application meet the criteria for approval. In doing so, the partnership was once again HUD and the developer, to the exclusion of the local citizens.

> Despite HUD's much ballyhooed ploy of involving local
> officials with their projects, Warren County officials are
> noticeable by their absence in planning for Soul City.
> "We've never been invited to participate in the planning
> of anything," says Frank W. Reams, an ex officio member
> of the County Planning Board and executive director of the
> County's Industrial Commission. "With enough money any-
> thing can happen," shrugs Claude T. Bowers, chairman of
> the governing board of county commissioners. Most resi-
> dents, he says, accept the project because "they realize
> that there is not too much they can do about it if (Uncle)
> Sam wants to do it."[17]

The reasons offered for federal disregarding and overriding of local citizen interests are valid: as in civil rights and housing legislation, some local citizens may be reactionary in their sentiments to the detriment of classes of the population the legislation is aimed at serving. New ideas themselves tend to provoke opposition from conservative local interests, but they will benefit from and appreciate the innovation in the long run. Title VII new communities fall into both categories—they are intended to benefit those classes of persons not served by conventional real estate development, and they represent a new and presumably improved life style.

Title VII, then, presents something of a dilemma in its role of protecting and enhancing the interest of the public. The program has shown itself to be willing and able to serve the interests of the Act and those of private developers, in a field where there is not sufficient demand in the absence of such a program. The program thus leads the local markets. But HUD is then in the position of responding to conditions and sensitivities of local areas all across the country, a responsibility that the SAR experience and others have indicated to be unfulfilled. The practice and impact of real estate development have traditionally been highly localized phenomena, not only because most developers are local but also because of the significant effects of residential and nonresidential development on local society, economy, and physical environment. What public controls there have been on real estate development have been local (except for national financial adjustments). The great developer abuses have also been local in origin and effect. Yet HUD has been assigned the responsibility for a program that cuts sharply into the local real estate market, with great impact on social, economic, and physical conditions, but without an adequate system of interpretation of local needs and balancing national and local objectives—except through the developer, HUD's partner. It is enough that HUD has the responsibility for such a major program—other federal programs are similarly assigned, but HUD has failed to formulate a workable mechanism for implementing the program given the myriad interests to be considered. If the Title VII program is so important that it necessitates the circumvention of potentially negative interests, then it is also important enough to have a systematic local citizen input into planning and development decisions. If this requires additional legislation, with greater (or different) economic incentives for developer participation in the program, then amendments to the Act should be sought.

In all fairness, there are some avenues for control already available for the introduction of state and local interests into the Title VII new community process. One type of control arrangement operates at the state level to represent public interests with respect to new community development. Since many of the most flagrant abuses, as well as the greatest overall number of new communities, have occurred in California and Arizona, those states have been prodded to enact legislation to protect future residents and surrounding communities from new community developers. Because of the fact that there have not as yet been any Title VII new communities in either state, the effects of such legislation on the Title VII implementation process are unknown.

Briefly, the California response to new community development has been fourfold: (1) enabling legislation for the creation of special districts as implementation mechanisms for new community development (in addition to existing use of utility and water districts); (2) establishment of Local Agency Formation Commissions for each county to rule on municipal incorporations and annexations; (3) expansion of the purview of the District Securities Commission to regulate bonds issued for new community development; and (4) more recently, passage of the California Environmental Quality Act, requiring environmental impact reports for new development projects. These state actions have been aimed primarily at protecting future residents and neighboring communities from excesses by developers in floating bonds to finance the development of new communities, as well as safeguarding society in general from environmental abuses. The measures have succeeded to a certain extent (and in some cases have led to greater problems, as in the case of Foster City), but have not addressed comprehensively the issue of the public interest in new community development. [18]

Another control mechanism, directly related to the federal level, is the A-95 review, in which local and regional governmental officials (and some private citizens) appraise the impact of all federally assisted actions. More will be said later in this chapter about the abilities of the COGs to represent local and regional public interests, but suffice it to conclude here that the A-95 review process is a valid and important exercise in control at the application stages of a project but is limited in the reactive nature of review as well as by COG composition and staff capabilities.

Citizen groups, as mentioned earlier, have increasingly challenged federal actions through resort to judicial review under NEPA and other legislation:

> NEPA does create, at the very least, a right to require
> compliance by the federal government with all of the Act's
> operative provisions. This right is one which citizen
> groups, functioning as private attorneys general, have
> standing to protect in the public interest. [19]

While such citizen power is at present somewhat restrained to procedural and limited substantive decision-making compliance with law by federal agencies, even a temporary delay in the case of projects like new communities can cause such a financial squeeze on private capital that the entire development can be jeopardized. As a result, citizen legal potential confers on certain groups with enough money and tenacity the power to damage or to kill Title VII projects which may or may not have complied perfectly with the law. Such power can be used to wring concessions from HUD and the developer that are tantamount to some measure of control over project implementation.

This type of citizen action, however, bestows the power to control disjointedly and possibly irrationally, not by systematic regulation. It is adequate to ameliorate some abuses in particular contexts, but the net effect is more anarchy than order. In San Antonio, a few groups and agencies were able to challenge and to delay temporarily the implementation of SAR, but the whole issue of controls for land development in critical areas and for federal program impacts could not be addressed because no means existed to do so. Even if there had been such, no mechanism was available for the reconciliation of the various factions with differing perceptions of the problems and solutions. Only HUD could probably have initiated the establishment of such local channels, as part of its new community implementation, and encouraged the effectuation of a systematic approach to new community involvement and evaluation on the local and regional levels.

Yet another major type of controls over new communities is being invoked against several conventional new communities by some local jurisdictions. This category involves reneging by a local government on previous agreements for provision of utilities or subdivision approval for a new community once under development. Such a nightmare for a developer has actually occurred in Maryland and Virginia. Original developer-government relations can easily deteriorate over a period of a few years, sometimes abetted by growing insularity of early new community residents and antagonism toward the developer or by new moods of growth suspension. In some cases the local governments are free to change the rules at will (city or county councils not bound by decisions of their predecessors); in others they are flaunting legal contracts for provision of sewer, water, and other services. In either event the developer is helpless in the face of such action, cannot continue to construct the community, and, even if it is a temporary halt while legal action is taken, can be bankrupted by the damage to his cash flow. This "control" may represent some public interests, but its invidiousness does not promote long-run public welfare. It is a serious problem for all concerned, and will probably occur in a Title VII situation before too long. It too represents anarchy rather than systematic regulation of developers and their new communities.

In sum, the problems of defining the representation for "the public interest" in Title VII new community development and of devising a HUD-developer-state and local government mechanism to regulate the development stem from fears of planners, developers, and administrators that citizen participation in the project would subvert the plan and complicate the implementation. The reluctance of real estate developers to bow to local governments is a long-standing tradition: they prefer to ignore or to co-opt the pertinent parts of the governments. And developers have never been overly concerned with the ultimate institutions or government that evolve in their developments. Now, under Title VII, a linkage is gradually being recognized between the interests of developers, of future residents, of neighboring communities, and of society in general (represented by HUD), but no mechanism has emerged to forge it. The same fears of citizen and governmental involvement persist.

The time dimension of new communities is perhaps the strongest argument for balanced and systematic participation in new community implementation. Not only do the impacts of a new community decision flow in wider and wider circles from the developer interests to those of society generally, but such decisions set in motion forces that greatly affect peoples' lives far into the future. Building a city is a momentous undertaking into which citizens with all their needs and desires cannot be dropped suddenly once some dwellings are completed. A developer, and his partner HUD, must recognize the continuity of planning, implementation, and operation. Citizen participation and governmental relations in the earliest stages smooth the way for proper governance of the new community once its residents assume control. Conversely, minimizing or controverting the former can lead to an undemocratic latter, that should not be the intention of any Federal program effort.

Essentially, the problems manifest in SAR and elsewhere imply a distrust by the developer and HUD of citizens and their elected officials in local communities. It is true that many local governments are inadequate to the tasks that confront them and that involvement in a new community can place a heavy strain on a local government. But can a federal program write off their participation as representatives of their citizenry on this basis alone? The New Communities Program, even as presently constituted, is a valuable and serious effort in the direction of improving large-scale real estate development and promoting by example a better way of life, if not to solve urban growth problems. The importance of this mission must not be disparaged by compromising the processes of citizen participation and governmental relations along the way. It can only be hoped that Title VII is a mandate for the federal government to foster a better way of life through encouraging local change rather than ignoring inconveniences.


NEW DIRECTIONS FOR NEW COMMUNITIES


There is no question that the New Communities Program has been evolving and changing ever since its inception. It could be clearly observed through the lengthy course of the SAR controversy: for example, neither environmental impact statements nor the concept of paired new communities were associated with Title VII when the SAR application was first submitted, but came to be important elements by the time the offer of commitment was made. Moreover, instead of the rush of developers to Title VII that was in progress in 1970, by 1972 the private sector was beginning to shy away, primarily because of procedural overloads: (1) HUD red tape and paperwork overloads, (2) difficulty in making timely decisions, (3) mandatory fiscal impact statements, (4) increasingly stiff A-95 review, and (5) requirements for social planning, as well as traditional physical and economic. By 1974 the Title VII program itself was besieged by problems of all sorts, including the funds freeze and other appropriations neglect, developer apathy and antagonisms, financial instability (and insolvency) of some already committed new communities (Cedar-Riverside, Jonathan, Riverton), and negative evaluations of the program from inside and outside sources. Thus not only is the New Communities Program itself quite different today from what it was when the SAR application was filed, but its very rationale for existence is being challenged from many sides. The time is right, therefore, for critical looks at what can be accomplished through the Title VII process that has been lacking in its short history to date. If the program is to be reconstituted, then valid changes should be included.

The following section of this study will put forth several proposals for altering the Title VII process with regard to control, representation, and governmental relations, based primarily on the problems indicated by the SAR case. The ideas are best viewed as policy guidelines for a new community development program: some would need further legislation, while others could be affected as HUD regulations. The final section will examine the viability of such amendments to the Title VII implementation process in terms of the overall state, regional, and local context in which the program must operate. The intent of the proposals is the creation of better new community development processes within a Title VII type of program, regardless of consequences for developer demand for the program. If such a program cannot generate enough developer interest or create economically sound new community projects, then the program and its incentives must be changed nationally, not the state and local governmental framework.

Modest Proposals for Title VII

Much has been said in this study of the problems and needs associated with new community development on the local level. Local governments of various types have had a rather poor record of affirmative action in the name of the public interest. One reason has stemmed from the ease with which real estate development interests have controlled local government structures for their own ends. Another is related to the limited powers of local governments (especially in Texas) to take strong, independent, innovative actions to solve developmental problems. A third reason results from financial weaknesses that have led to greater and greater dependence on, and consequent obeisance to, federal programs.

Together, such limitations of local governments (including counties, municipalities, and districts) provide strong fuel for arguments that only at the state level can new community, as well as wider land development, controls be effectively introduced.

> State governments are the ultimate sources of the police
> power, which supports our system of local land use control.
> It is obvious, however, that local government cannot cope
> with all the problems presented by the new communities.
> If other measures fail, the states may be forced to restruc-
> ture the basis of land use control and to permit state or
> regional guidance of large-scale development. [20]

By aiming at the state level, however, particularly in a state as large as Texas, the whole apparent need for responsiveness to the subtleties of the public interest is significantly compromised. In Texas also, the SAR experience does not encourage faith in the administrative structure or operations as the most effective stratum for innovative controls. Regional agencies are little better, since they, at least for the present, are either single-purpose entities or lack political constituencies, being composed instead of officials elected from other governments.

In the case of Title VII, HUD and the federal government are the ultimate effectuators, who presumably will be responsible for any additions or changes in new community development programs or processes not forthcoming on state or local initiative. Indeed, the carrots and sticks of federal policy might well have to be relied upon for inducing changes in state and local policy. Federal origination permits some flexibility in creating combinations of controls for the several levels of government, taking advantage of the state as the sovereign legal being, but avoiding the pitfalls of merely introducing another unresponsive department or board to smother the interests of the local publics.

The type of governmental relations changes in the Title VII process suggested by the SAR experience generally concern citizen and governmental involvement in planning, review, and control of new community development. Such involvement would have to occur at an early stage in the proposed project, and would include a specific series of analyses related to the impact of the new community, from which independent judgments could be made. The final output would be the transformation of citizen involvement into a system of governance for the new community. In addition, local governments would need the resources (and perhaps the stimulation) to carry on collateral developmental activities to blend the new community in with the existing area.

The first step might be the creation on the state level of a new communities commission, which would consist of permanent appointed members (supplemented perhaps temporarily by additional members who are residents of the county in which any new community under discussion is located), and which would be vested with the responsibility of determining whether creation of any new community is in the public interest. As an ongoing function, the commission could carry out studies and adopt regulations related to: (1) criteria for the types of new communities to fall under its jurisdiction; (2) specific guidelines for the implementation process it would oversee, for both Title VII and non-Title VII new communities; (3) generalized sites for new communities within the state; and (4) capabilities of metropolitan planning and government to respond to a new community project in its area. Once in full operation, the commission would review new community proposals to HUD (and all others) on the basis of impact on the metropolitan area, impact on the county and municipalities, tax base of the new community, provision for existing residents of the site, if any, and other criteria. The commission could be required to solicit opinion in various quarters of the local area regarding the new community, but not necessarily to abide by the results. Also, the commission would set up and administer the mechanism for instituting a local government, especially sensitive in the transfer from developer to citizens, as well as insure the proper provision of all public services, such as schools, sewers, parks, and police.

None of the above duties of the commission would necessarily conflict with HUD responsibilities under Title VII, unless the commission stopped a new community HUD was reviewing as favorable on its criteria. The commission concept provides a solid foundation to a multifaceted new communities program, by lodging final review authority and implementation monitoring in the state, where ultimate police power and sovereignty reside. A couple of obvious drawbacks are that the state level (especially in large states) can also be unresponsive to local conditions and that the commission is as vulnerable as any state agency to political influence which might or might not imperil the goals of the commission (if SAR is any guide, such goals would indeed be in jeopardy). Since such politicking on the state level does not effectively reconcile local interests, the commission must be supplemented with other mechanisms.

The key element in the overall new community implementation program would be a special board or authority established for each new community by the state commission. On the primary level, this board would be the action arm of the state commission in actually carrying out most of its functions, although the policy and final decision powers in such matters would remain with the commission. These functions include reviewing the proposal and plans for the new community (since creation of the board would be required prior to submittal of a Final Application to HUD), soliciting opinion in the local area concerning the new community, and instituting the new community government and public services. In addition, HUD would be able to utilize the board to fund detailed studies of special problems or aspects of the new community and its impact as needed, or as the board or commission requested.

In composition, the board would be analogous to the Water Quality Advisory Review Board for SAR, except that it would consist of elected officials for the most part. The state commission would submit to HUD a list of governmental entities and agencies to be represented on the board, with the appropriate staff support; HUD would issue invitations to join this board. Whatever the total number of voting agencies represented on the board, the developer team would initially be granted an equal number less one of votes in all policy matters. All decisions of the board would be subject to review and remand by the state commission.

The local board would function as the implementing and coordinating arm of local and metropolitan planning for the area. Much closer than the state commission and HUD to local planning considerations, the board would be more able to interpret comprehensive and categorical planning already done, and in process, with respect to the overall new community proposal and its specific project components, both in the review phase and during implementation. The board would also be in a position to request or to commission further planning studies by public agencies as it perceived the need. This entire area was critically lacking in the SAR case.

The board would also act as a countervailing political force to the state commission, and more resistant to political pressures, because of the great diversity of its membership. The board, composed of many agency representatives, would be difficult enough to influence on any issue, but beyond the board would lie the state commission, which presumably would be subject to different political pressures. No mechanism is not subject to political influence, but this proposed structure channelizes the political conflict and brings it into open view. In this way the issues surrounding a new community could be effectively defused (in the sense that SAR was explosive).

Further elaborations on the outline of local board duties might include (1) bonding authority for the board to plan and execute public works and facilities in conjunction with the new community development but not part of it, (2) designation of the board as the public agency to which federal infrastructure and other grants would be made for the new community, thus creating a coordinating function for the board, and (3) expansion of the board's responsibilities to include sponsorship and development of low and moderate income housing within the new community. In addition, the state commission could ultimately become a development authority or corporation patterned to some degree after the powers of the New York State Urban Development Corporation, which has been active in large new community development within Title VII.

Assuming the recommended changes to have been instituted, the governmental relations process of the Title VII new communities program could operate as follows. A permanent state commission on new communities would presumably be in existence already. A developer assembles his land and prepares his plans, in consultation with HUD and with notification to the state commission. The Pre-Application is submitted and work initiated on the Final Application. At the time of its submittal, the developer files an application with the state commission for approval of the formation of a new community district at the site, supported by plans, documentation, and environmental and fiscal impact statements. The state commission thereupon convenes a local board for the new community (with HUD's concurrence and/or invitations), and with its assistance carries out a detailed review of the proposal, based on specific written criteria previously prepared, approximately concurrently with the normal A-95 review and during the HUD application review. Formal meetings of the local board are to be open to the public, functioning as public hearings on the new community proposal. The local board reviews the proposal on the basis of compatibility with local and metropolitan planning, impact on the surrounding land and metropolitan area, desirability of the site location, accessibility, public facilities included and required, magnitude of potential environmental hazards, ability and willingness of cognizant jurisdictions to service the community, and other factors relating to the local area. Such review is intended to complement and improve HUD review, rather than to supersede it or to obviate it. Since this local review does encompass some of the A-95 standards and participants, it is possible that a properly constituted local board could eventually be granted A-95 review authority for new communities.

The local board forwards the results of its review to the state commission, which in turn transmits its verdict to HUD. Assuming a favorable recommendation from the state commission, and from the

HUD staff, the Community Development Corporation in HUD could then authorize an offer of commitment to the developer.

Once the offer of commitment to guarantee the new community under Title VII has been made and accepted, the local board for the new community becomes formally and permanently constituted, with public agency and developer representatives, and with appropriate staff. This board is the precursor to a system of governance for the new community, but at the earliest stages represents many citizen interests in the area, as well as those of future residents. It is involved (together with the responsible governmental jurisdictions) in most major decisions pertaining to the new community implementation, including all legal zoning, subdivision, water, sewer, transportation, and public works approvals, serving as grantee for federal assistance, funding studies and projects as required, planning for the future government, and monitoring developer activities along with HUD. The board is not to be involved, except on an advisory basis, in selecting builders and contractors, in marketing, and in any area not legally sanctioned locally or included in the development plan (such as urban design controls). The duties and responsibilities of the local board and of its parent state commission are to be included in the project agreement executed between HUD and the developer as part of the Title VII program. Any changes therein at a future time will be cleared through the same local and state review process as occurred originally.

The most cogent criticism of the proposals made in this section would be that they are redundant and frivolous when COGs and other regional clearing-houses exist already with structure and functions not markedly different. The greatest strengths of the COGs in general are that they are regional in nature, that they bring together elected officials, staff, and citizens of many jurisdictions, and that the valuable A-95 review authority has been conferred on them by the federal government. However, for new community development involvement, many weaknesses are also apparent, as demonstrated during the course of the SAR debate within AACOG. The main argument against COGs is their close ties to the federal government, and especially to HUD as their chief funding agent. With such financial links, independent review and strong initiative might be difficult to maintain in the face of HUD commitments to its new community projects. The need is for countervailing political forces deriving from the state, not for one federal arm evaluating another. In addition, COG memberships and voting distributions tend to favor suburban and rural interests versus the larger cities, thus encouraging some types of issues and decisions over others. Furthermore, COGs for the most part are oriented toward regional planning rather than developmental and regulatory planning, which are the fortes of city and county agencies.

Lastly, COGs have little experience in managing, even by delegation, programs of an ongoing nature like new community development.

At least one state has moved ahead already on its own in passing legislation implementing some of the above proposals. In June 1972 the Ohio legislature enacted a law providing for the establishment of new community authorities for Title VII projects. The county within which the new community is proposed to be located sets up the authority after approval is granted the new community through a public hearing. The county appoints three to six members, to represent county citizens and future residents of the new community, and one member to represent the local municipality, if any. The developer appoints an equal number of representatives. Appointed members of the authority of all types are gradually replaced by elected new community residents as the population level of the community rises, until the authority is entirely elective.

The authority, a compromise between developer and public interests, has no power over zoning and subdivisions, water and sewer extension, and police and fire protection, but has a broad role in public facilities, planning, and public land development, backed up by taxing, bond issuance, land acquisition, and contractual powers. The authority can be dissolved in a referendum of new community residents. It is clearly a mechanism that is intended to complement, rather than to supplant, a municipal government. Citizens of the area are involved fairly early in the process (at the time of the HUD guarantee), yet are not able to circumvent the developer's plans.[21]

The proposals set forth in this chapter for both the local new community boards and the state commissions are also middle-of-the-road compromises, and are operable within the existing Title VII framework, aiming to establish a formal structure and process of state and local regulation of developer (and HUD) initiative. But at the same time the proposed schema is very flexible and is not at all limited to the Title VII program. The activities of the board and commission could fall in any part of a continuum from the present situation of developer initiative in partnership with HUD to a future condition of governmental initiative in which the state commission would decide on a new community project and create a local board to develop it (British model). The proposals are also as applicable to state-sponsored legislation as to federally induced changes in new communities development, as discussed in greater detail in the next section.

Effectuation and Effects

Much has been said throughout this study concerning the role of the federal government in change. Title VII, as a federal program, can also be a powerful stimulant to change on the state and local levels. The SAR experience introduces some convincing arguments that the Title VII program as presently constituted and administered has many weaknesses, which, given the enormous impact of large new communities on local areas and future residents, are quite dangerous as long as they persist. Many of these weaknesses, however, appear to be correctible within the general Title VII structure, thus enabling the continuation of this partnership approach to new community development as a beginning step toward a more comprehensive program linked to overall urban and rural growth and development policy.

The New Communities Program can be used as an inducement to effect the changes proposed in this chapter for state and local participation in the program. Few of these changes, either structural or procedural, are likely to materialize on the initiative of the various states through their own enabling legislation: Ohio was a notable exception even in the limited Act it passed in 1972. Although additional congressional action would be desirable in establishing a new mandate for the New Communities Program, the necessary changes in the program can be made within HUD—revising the Title VII program and its administration, and using the Title VII emoluments and clients to induce state and local activity along lines described below.

At the highest and most desirable policy level, the New Communities Program legislation itself could be amended by Congress to emphasize an intergovernmental partnership along with the private-public partnership. The legislation should call for the creation of new communities commissions at the state level and require local boards for all new communities under Title VII as a prerequisite for approval. In addition, basic to any intergovernmental provisions, financial assistance should be authorized (and eventually appropriated) to states for use in the formation and operation of commissions, and to local boards once created for certain types of planning and administrative activities. As a greater inducement, various curtailments of other assistance (such as 701 Planning Assistance) to states could be mandated to encourage compliance with the provisions of the legislation. In effect, such actions would amount to federal instigation of the means through which state and local areas would be able to protect themselves from overzealous federal bureaucratic intrusions in the future—a laudable purpose for federal legislation.

At the second level, HUD needs to change its regulations (and eventually finalize them) for the New Communities Program, in recognition of the evolution that new community development has undergone within the past few years. Such changes should include (1) unequivocal restatement of criteria of eligibility for new community projects under the Title VII objectives, (2) clear statement of impact assessments and governmental relations to be required of private developers,

(3) emphasis on greater input from the state and local levels (and even from HUD regional and area offices), and (4) different criteria and processes for each of the different types of new communities.

Clearly, the first and second recommendations above are merely intended to codify products of the rapid evolution of Title VII toward somewhat more responsible HUD stewardship for the wide variety of public interests in new community development (at least partially due to the SAR experience). The program has in fact changed, and the new status should be reflected in the regulations for all to see. The third recommendation above includes at the very least the formation of an ad hoc assemblage of local and regional governments to review continuously each new community. But optimally the creation of state new communities commissions and local boards should be encouraged or required, either through congressional mandate or HUD inducement (described in greater detail below). Finally, different new community types should be abetted by HUD, but each in its own way. A new town in-town is as unlike a satellite new community as regional planning is to Model Cities. New towns in-town, for example, essentially represent an advanced technique of urban renewal in which private sector initiative and management are little more than a cover for the inadequacies of urban renewal agencies. Unlike other new communities, the developer is not tied to one site in his initiative, and there is little chance of a unified, self-sufficient community resulting from the efforts (indeed, if it did, it could be destructive to the host city). Other types have similar but less striking idiosyncrasies.

Thirdly, HUD can alter its administration of Title VII better to achieve program objectives, including state and local governmental innovations. Even without congressional amendment of the New Communities Program, HUD has many options available to it in implementing the governmental relations proposals set forth earlier in this chapter. For example, the potential financial resources of the current Title VII program could be sufficient "carrots" to stir several state legislatures into action in the creation of new communities commissions with suitably defined duties and responsibilities. HUD personnel could assist in the drafting of the necessary legislation according to its own model. In addition, HUD's leverage with supplicant private developers, who normally have significant political clout in their communities and states, could be utilized to further stimulate such action. Furthermore, HUD could insist (as ultimately with SAR) that no new community could be approved under Title VII until a properly constituted local board is formed and reviews the project plans.

Finally, HUD could orient other programs within the Department to the attainment of objectives of the New Communities Program. Assistance grants (such as 701 Planning Assistance), for example, could be keyed to advance planning for new communities or earmarked for local new community boards once formed. Review and implementation of new communities under Title VII would be considerably easier and more effective if comprehensive planning had been carried out in advance by local and regional agencies. This planning might include the analysis of future growth and development, identification of growth management strategies, and recommendation of alternative sites where new development could be concentrated in the form of new communities—optimal sites with respect to the area's needs and resources. Eligibility of local new community boards (as well as state commissions) for assistance programs should be a strong incentive for their creation, with functions HUD would have a voice in determining. Once again, through the use of carrots and sticks, the federal level would be inducing mechanisms through which states and local areas would become more powerful in their federal relations in the future.

The process that will result from the above improvements in the New Communities Program will permit great progress toward alleviation of many problems that arose during the SAR governmental relations, and toward better achievement of the program objectives. The most serious single problem of SAR was the conspiratorial manner in which the developer and HUD made decisions and strategy, in furtherance of the SAR project implementation, but to the detriment of important elements of the public interest. Any opportunities for substantial participation in the planning or review, even by professional staff personnel of local agencies, were single-meeting public exposures such as the AACOG A-95 review. The structural and procedural changes in governmental relations for new communities proposed in this chapter provided for a mechanism which will facilitate a broad-based and continuous involvement of local and regional public officials, as the surrogates for real citizen participation in the process, which is probably too chaotic and expensive to be feasible in the Title VII context.

Under the proposals, the developers retain the ability to protect and fulfill their interests in the new community, with few additional responsibilities and little extra time delay. Generally, the proposed changes involve a transfer of review authority on certain matters from HUD to the new state and local bodies. HUD can accomplish its statutory obligations better because the proposed process will to a greater degree

> encourage the orderly development of well-planned . . . new communities . . . ; strengthen the capacity of state and local governments to deal with local problems; preserve and enhance both the natural and urban environment.[22]

The interests of surrounding citizens will be furthered by the participation of representatives of local public agencies on the new community board, while the interests of future residents of the new community will be protected by the involvement of local officials and the early seating of elected residents on the board as it evolves into a government for the new community.

## SAR, New Communities, and the Future

New community development and the Title VII program have evolved considerably in the past few years. Private developers now face a greatly magnified set of problems in any new community project—partially due to unfavorable economic conditions, but also as a result of heightened citizen and governmental militancy against the new, the large, and the unknown in their areas. The Title VII program represents even greater problems for new community developers because of restrictions and requirements imposed by HUD, the potential for lengthy delays, and increased vulnerability to destruction by actions of local private and public groups. HUD's response to changing needs in new community development has actually been a greater sense of responsibility for the interests of many publics, but manifested through more requirements, more documentation, longer delays, and tighter controls. The motivation toward the public trust has been there, but the effect has been to dampen interest in and effectiveness of the program.

SAR acted as a turning point and bellwether in the process of change for Title VII. Reviewed at an early stage in the program, and finally litigated recently, SAR represented the worst in political maneuvering and conspiratorial conduct at various levels of government, was the first Title VII new community whose legal right to be developed was tested and upheld, and was, more than any other single cause, responsible for the changes in HUD's requirements and its attitudes toward its role as public trustee vis-a-vis new communities. Since the SAR controversy, new communities have had great, sometimes insurmountable, problems with citizens and local governments—plans for several have had to be abandoned. The SAR case has left a bitter legacy in one city, and has helped bring a virtual halt to the Title VII program; but, ironically, just as the SAR debate may have great long-run benefits for the people of San Antonio, so also may the New Communities Program ultimately be better off for its crisis.

Today the trend of federal programs overall is one of decentralization and participation. But Title VII runs directly contrary to that trend. Now immobilized by economics and politics, the Title VII program must be adapted to current conditions and emerging governmental roles. The most pressing need is for increasing the incentives for the private sector in the program, to balance the stronger voice to be maintained by HUD in the private-public partnership. But at the same time the New Communities Program can be an important vehicle for inducing the establishment of permanent processes on the state and local levels which will be working to achieve the objectives of the program. Decentralization in this instance means using federal initiative to create the mechanisms, multiplied across the country, by which federal policy can to a greater extent be realized. Effectuation of the proposals for state commissions and local boards will also increase participation in the implementation of new communities, thereby lowering the probability for disaster in governmental or legal action against new communities. The valid objectives of the New Communities Program can actually be realized to a greater extent today than in 1970, due to the gradual (and sometimes enforced) evolution in HUD's perception of, and reaction to, its role in the partnership approach to new community development. Now HUD has the responsibility as warden of the Title VII program to work to effect new and better processes for new community implementation throughout the federal-state-local structure.

The New Communities Program challenges experts because it impacts strongly on the basic systems of peoples' lives: people will live, work, and play in new communities, and in a particular style related to their design and operation. Nothing could be more important as a responsibility of the public than to ensure that this program is optimally constituted. Nothing can help ensure this more than the broad involvement of the many interests of citizens in the new community development process. The public interest is not singular and defies precise definition, but it cannot be protected and enhanced by a federal-private partnership alone. The New Communities Program can be broadened in the direction of state and local area interests without compromising its goals or its products. It may represent only a beginning in policy for urban growth and development, but it can become a significant step in marshaling total resources—federal, state, local, and private—that will be needed for a massive effort. Change will move the program further in that direction, and that is the direction of the future.

NOTES

1. Robert E. Simon, Jr., "New Communities in the Seventies, Part II: Riverton, New York," in Shirley F. Weiss, Edward J. Kaiser, and Raymond J. Burby III, eds., New Community Development:

119

Planning Process, Implementation, and Emerging Social Concerns, Vol. 2 (Chapel Hill, N.C.: New Towns Research Seminar, Center for Urban and Regional Studies, University of North Carolina at Chapel Hill, 1971), pp. 191-92.

2. Although evidence to the contrary, based on admittedly limited research in Title VII new communities, has emerged from the recent work of the Center for Urban and Regional Studies, University of North Carolina, "Performance Criteria for New Community Development: Evaluation and Prognosis."

3. Housing and Urban Development Act of 1970, P.L. 91-609, Title VII, Sec. 712(a); 42 U.S.C. 4513(a).

4. John G. Gliege, New Towns: Policy Problems in Regulating Development, Papers in Public Administration No. 17 (Tempe, Ariz.: Institute for Public Administration, Arizona State University, 1970), p. 131.

5. HUD Draft Regulations: Assistance for New Communities (Urban Growth and New Community Development Act of 1970), 24 CFR 720 (August 7, 1972), Sec. 720.13(e).

6. Robert H. Ryan, "New Towns and Public Policy," in Weiss, et al., op. cit., Vol. 1, p. 139.

7. Simon, op. cit., p. 202.

8. Stanley Scott, "Local Government and the New Communities," Public Affairs Report, Institute of Governmental Studies, University of California, Berkeley, Vol. 6, No. 3 (June 1965), p. 2.

9. Donald J. Bodnar and Mark Wassenich, Implementation: A Critical Limit on the Planner's Role in Planned Community Development, Research Memorandum (Chapel Hill, N.C.: Center for Urban and Regional Studies, University of North Carolina at Chapel Hill, 1970), pp. 8-9.

10. Ibid., p. 9.

11. Anthony J. Mumphrey, Jr., John E. Seley, and Julian Wolpert, "A Decision Model for Locating Controversial Facilities," Journal of the American Institute of Planners, Vol. 37, No. 6 (November 1971), p. 397.

12. Scott, op. cit., pp. 4-5.

13. Theories and analyses of this process are numerous. See, for example, David B. Truman, The Governmental Process, (New York: Alfred A. Knopf, 1955).

14. Stanley Scott, New Towns Development and the Role of Government, Institute of Governmental Studies, University of California, Berkeley, 1964 (unpublished), p. 33.

15. See Francis E. Rourke, Bureaucracy, Politics, and Public Policy (Boston: Little, Brown and Co., 1969).

16. Lawrence Meyer, "County Coolness Imperils New Town," Washington Post, January 10, 1972.

17. Bill McAllister, "A 'Soul City' In the Carolina Piedmont," Norfolk Virginian-Pilot, July 16, 1972.

18. Gliege, op. cit., pp. 40-44.

19. Bernard S. Cohen and Jacqueline Manney Warren, "Judicial Recognition of the Substantive Requirements of the National Environmental Policy Act of 1969," Boston College Industrial and Commercial Law Review, Vol. 13, No. 4 (March 1972), p. 688.

20. Stanley Scott, "The Large New Communities and Urban Growth: A Broader Perspective and Its Implications," Public Affairs Report, Institute of Governmental Studies, University of California, Berkeley, Vol. 6, No. 6 (December 1965), p. 5.

21. See Paul O'Mara, "Citizen Participation Sought in New Towns," Planning, Vol. 38, No. 11 (December 1972), pp. 300-02.

22. Housing and Urban Development Act of 1970, P. L. 91-609, Title VII, Sec. 710(f); 42 U.S.C. 4511(f).

## APPENDIX

Richard D. Broun, Deputy Director, Office of Community and Environmental Standards, Department of Housing and Urban Development.

Edmund D. Cody, Superintendent, Northside Independent School District.

James E. Collier, New Communities Liaison Officer, Region VI, Department of Housing and Urban Development.

Edward F. Davis, Director of Planning, City of San Antonio.

Georgia K. Davis, Editor, Urban Life in New and Renewing Communities.

Anthony P. DeVito, Application Review Division, Office of New Communities, Department of Housing and Urban Development.

F. Clement Dinsmore, Attorney Advisor, Office of the General Counsel, Department of Housing and Urban Development.

John Gatti, Mayor, City of San Antonio.

Mel A. Goodwin, Regional Planner, Alamo Area Council of Governments.

Edmond Harvey, City of San Antonio Public Service Board.

Charles H. Hembree, Federal Assistance Branch, Region VI, Environmental Protection Agency.

Dr. Robert L.M. Hilliard, City Councilman, City of San Antonio.

Bernard J. Hoffnar, (former) Senior Associate, Gladstone Associates.

Robert G. Honts, Partner, Christian, Miller, and Honts; Managing Partner, San Antonio Ranch, Ltd.

M.M. (Mel) Hughes, Chairman, Planning and Zoning Commission, City of San Antonio.

Charles O. Kilpatrick, Publisher, San Antonio Express and News.

Philip D. LeMessurier, Chairman, South Texas Group, The Sierra Club.

M. Winston Martin, Executive Director, San Antonio Development Agency.

J. Timothy O'Reilly, Vice President, Gladstone Associates.

Albert A. Pena, Jr., County Commissioner, Bexar County.

Fred N. Pfeiffer, Manager, San Antonio River Authority.

Blair Reeves, County Judge, Bexar County.

Jill Root, President, League of Women Voters.

Louis T. Rosenberg, Attorney.

Robert Sohn, President, Citizens for a Better Environment.
Dr. Arleigh B. Templeton, President, University of Texas, San Antonio.
Richard G. Toler, Operations Manager, City of San Antonio Water Board.
Felix B. Trevino, (former) City Councilman, City of San Antonio.
Otis M. Trimble, Environmental Clearance Officer, Region VI, Department of Housing and Urban Development.
Arthur C. Troilo, Jr., (former) Director, Office of Community and Environmental Standards, Department of Housing and Urban Development.
Frank Vaughan, County Commissioner, Bexar County.
Sherry K. Wagner, Consultant.
Col. McDonald D. Weinert, General Manager, Edwards Underground Water District.
Char White, Former President, Citizens for a Better Environment.
Hugh C. Yantis, Jr., Executive Director, Texas Water Quality Board.

---

Note: All interviews were personally conducted between August and November 1972, in San Antonio, Austin, and Fort Worth, Tex., Columbia, Md., and Washington, D.C. Listed affiliations were those at the time of the interview (except as otherwise noted).

# BIBLIOGRAPHY

San Antonio Ranch


Beck, Henry V. An Evaluation of Water Quality Studies on San Antonio Ranch New Town, submitted to Office of New Community Development, Department of Housing and Urban Development, August 19, 1972.

Bexar County Commissioners Court. Resolution, opposing development over the Edwards Aquifer, November 12, 1971.

"The Big Troubles at San Antonio Ranch." Business Week, November 3, 1973, pp. 78-79.

Christian, Miller, and Honts, Inc. Report to the Alamo Area Council of Governments, San Antonio Ranch, April 20, 1971.

____. Special Report for the Board of Directors, Community Development Corporation, September 15, 1971.

____. Special Report to Assistant Secretary Samuel Jackson, September 28, 1971.

____. Special Report for the City Council, City of San Antonio, November 4, 1971.

Dugger, Ronnie. "New Towns, Old Politics," The Texas Observer, May 25, 1973; "New Towns: 1 Up, 1 Down," The Texas Observer, June 29, 1973; "One New Town and the City Council," The Texas Observer, July 13, 1973.

Edwards Underground Water District, Resolution, opposing development over the Edwards Aquifer, December 15, 1971.

Gladstone Associates. Preliminary Economic Feasibility Study for San Antonio Ranch, March 1970.

\_\_\_\_. Market Potentials and Development Program, San Antonio Ranch New Town, November 1970.

\_\_\_\_. San Antonio Ranch New Town Research and Development Program Potentials, May 27, 1971.

Hill, Bob. "Comments on the Special Report by L.J. Turk to the San Antonio Ranch Water Quality Advisory Review Board Dated May 11, 1972," TWQB Interoffice Memorandum, June 1, 1972.

"New Town," series of eight articles on San Antonio Ranch, in San Antonio Light, March 19-27, 1971.

Pereira, William L. Associates. San Antonio Ranch—A University Community Study, October 1969; revised March 1970.

\_\_\_\_. Master Plan for San Antonio Ranch, November 1970.

San Antonio City Council. Resolution No. 72-7-9, generally approving San Antonio Ranch plan and expressing intent to annex, February 10, 1972.

\_\_\_\_. Agreement, between the City of San Antonio and San Antonio Ranch, Ltd., Ordinance No. 40358, February 3, 1972; amended, Ordinance No. 40397, February 17, 1972.

San Antonio Ranch, Ltd. Final Application, submitted to U.S. Department of Housing and Urban Development, November 12, 1970; amended May 13, 1971, et seq.

\_\_\_\_. Special Report for the City Council, City of San Antonio, November 29, 1971.

\_\_\_\_. Selected Design Criteria, Construction Standards, and Procedures Concerning Water Quality on San Antonio Ranch, Special Report to the San Antonio Ranch Water Quality Advisory Review Board, June 23, 1972.

San Antonio River Authority, Resolution, opposing development over the Edwards Aquifer, December 15, 1971.

Sierra Club v. Lynn, 364 F.Supp. 834 (W.D. Texas, 1973).

Sierra Club v. Lynn, 502 F. 2d 43 (5th Cir., 1974).

Spears, Adrian A. Order (March 14, 1972), Sierra Club, et al. v. George W. Romney, et al., U.S. District Court, Western District of Texas, San Antonio Division.

_____. Order (March 7, 1973), Sierra Club, et al. v. George W. Romney, et al., U.S. District Court, Western District of Texas, San Antonio Division.

_____. Judgment and Order (May 21, 1973), Sierra Club, et al. v. James T. Lynn, et al., U.S. District Court, Western District of Texas, San Antonio Division.

_____. Order and Memorandum Opinion (August 24, 1973), Sierra Club, et al. v. James T. Lynn, et al., U.S. District Court, Western District of Texas, San Antonio Division.

Texas Water Quality Board. Order No. 71-1216-24, approving plans for San Antonio Ranch New Town, December 16, 1971.

_____. Order No. 72-0628-20, approving the studies for the San Antonio Ranch Water Quality Advisory Review Board, June 30, 1972.

Turk, L.J. Water Quality and Geological Mapping Studies, Special Reports to the San Antonio Ranch Water Quality Advisory Review Board, April 24, 1972, May 11, 1972, and June 8, 1972.

Turk, L.J., and E. Gus Fruh. Water Quality and Geological Studies, Summary Report to the San Antonio Ranch Water Quality Advisory Review Board, June 23, 1972.

U.S. Department of Housing and Urban Development, "HUD Guarantee of Texas New Town Contingent Upon Water Protection Studies," HUD News, No. 72-131, February 28, 1972.

_____. Draft Environmental Impact Statement on Proposed New Community of San Antonio Ranch, Bexar County, Texas, September 13, 1971.

_____. Final Environmental Impact Statement on Proposed New Community of San Antonio Ranch, Bexar County, Texas, January 20, 1972.

_____. Addendum to Final Environmental Impact Statement on Proposed New Community of San Antonio Ranch, Bexar County, Texas, August 24, 1972.

Winslow, D. E., and W. H. Espey, Jr. Storm Water Runoff Volume and Recharge Analysis for the San Antonio Ranch, submitted by TRACOR, Inc., June 19, 1972.

San Antonio Express and News (miscellaneous articles), San Antonio, Tex.

San Antonio Light (miscellaneous articles), San Antonio, Tex.


Political and Governmental


Advisory Commission on Intergovernmental Relations, Impact of Federal Urban Development Programs on Local Government Organization and Planning (Washington, D. C.: U.S. Senate, Committee on Government Operations, 88th Cong., 2nd Sess., January 1964).

Advisory Commission on Intergovernmental Relations, Role of the Federal Government in Metropolitan Areas (Washington, D. C.: The Commission, December 1962).

Agger, Robert E., Daniel Goldrich, and Bert E. Swanson. The Rulers and the Ruled (New York: John Wiley & Sons, 1964).

Alford, Robert R. Bureaucracy and Participation (Chicago: Rand McNally & Co., 1969).

Altshuler, Alan A. The City Planning Process: A Political Analysis (Ithaca, N. Y.: Cornell University Press, 1965).

Anderson, Martin. The Federal Bulldozer (Cambridge, Mass.: The M.I.T. Press, 1964).

Bachrach, Peter, and Morton S. Baratz. "Decisions and Nondecisions: An Analytical Framework," American Political Science Review, Vol. 57, No. 3 (September 1963), pp. 632-42.

____. Power and Poverty: Theory and Practice (New York: Oxford University Press, 1970).

Banfield, Edward C., and James Q. Wilson. City Politics (Cambridge, Mass.: Harvard University Press, 1963).

Benton, Wilbourn E. Texas: Its Government and Politics, 2nd ed. (Englewood Cliffs, N.J.: Prentice-Hall, Inc., 1966).

Benveniste, Guy. The Politics of Expertise (Berkeley, Calif.: The Glendessary Press, 1972).

Clark, Terry N., ed. Community Structure and Decision-Making: Comparative Analyses (San Francisco: Chandler Publishing Co., 1968).

Cobb, Roger W., and Charles D. Elder. Participation in American Politics: The Dynamics of Agenda-Building (Boston: Allyn and Bacon, Inc., 1972).

Cohen, Bernard S., and Jacqueline Manney Warren. "Judicial Recognition of the Substantive Requirements of the National Environmental Policy Act of 1969," Boston College Industrial and Commercial Law Review, Vol. 13, No. 4 (March 1972), pp. 685-704.

Comptroller General of the U.S. Improvements Needed in Federal Efforts to Implement the National Environmental Policy Act of 1969, Report to the Subcommittee on Fisheries and Wildlife Conservation, House Committee on Merchant Marine and Fisheries (Washington, D.C.: Government Accounting Office, May 18, 1972).

Council on Environmental Quality. Statements on Proposed Federal Actions Affecting the Environment, 40 CFR 1500, 36 Fed. Reg. 7724 (April 23, 1971); Guidelines for Preparation of Environmental Impact Statements, 38 Fed. Reg. 20551 (August 1, 1973).

Cox, Kevin. Conflict, Power, and Politics in the City: A Geographic View (New York: McGraw-Hill, Inc., 1973).

Dahl, Robert A. Who Governs? Democracy and Power in an American City (New Haven: Yale University Press, 1961).

Downs, Anthony. An Economic Theory of Democracy (New York: Harper & Row, Publishers, 1957).

Dugger, Ronnie. Our Invaded Universities: Form, Reform, and New Starts (New York: W.W. Norton & Co., 1974).

Durchslag, Melvyn R., and Peter D. Junger. "HUD and the Human Environment: A Preliminary Analysis of the Impact of the National

Environmental Policy Act of 1969 upon the Department of Housing and Urban Development," Iowa Law Review, Vol. 58, No. 4 (April 1973), pp. 805-90.

Easton, David, ed. Varieties of Political Power (Englewood Cliffs, N.J.: Prentice-Hall, Inc., 1966).

Elazar, Daniel J. "Fragmentation and Local Organizational Responses to Federal-City Programs," Urban Affairs Quarterly, Vol. 2, No. 4 (June 1967), pp. 30-46.

Endres, Mary Ellen. "Environmental Protection: Citizen Action Forcing Agency Compliance Under Limited Judicial Review," St. Mary's Law Journal, Vol. 6, No. 2 (Summer 1974), pp. 421-43.

Epstein, Edwin M. The Corporation in American Politics (Englewood Cliffs, N.J.: Prentice-Hall, Inc., 1969).

Fellmeth, Robert C. The Politics of Land (New York: Grossman Publishers, 1973).

Fisher, Francis D. "The Carrot and the Stick: Conditions for Federal Assistance," Harvard Journal on Legislation, Vol. 6, No. 4 (May 1969), pp. 401-12.

Frey, Frederick W. "Comment: On Issues and Nonissues in the Study of Power," American Political Science Review, Vol. 65, No. 4 (December 1971), pp. 1081-1101.

Gantt, Fred Jr., Irving Owen Dawson, and Luther G. Hagard, Jr., eds. Governing Texas: Documents and Readings, 2nd ed. (New York: Thomas Y. Crowell Co., 1970).

Goodall, Leonard E., ed. Urban Politics in the Southwest (Tempe, Ariz.: Institute of Public Administration, Arizona State University, 1967).

Hawley, Willis D., ed. Where Governments Meet: Emerging Patterns of Intergovernmental Relations (Berkeley, Cal.: Institute of Governmental Studies, University of California, 1967).

Held, Virginia. The Public Interest and Individual Interests (New York: Basic Books, Inc., 1970).

Henson, John, and Stephen M. Vaughan. "The University of Texas at San Antonio Site Acquisition Study," for the Legal Research Project, University of Texas at Austin, September 5, 1971.

Hunter, Floyd. Community Power Structure: A Study of Decision Makers (Chapel Hill: University of North Carolina Press, 1953).

Key, V.O., Jr. Politics, Parties, and Pressure Groups (New York: Thomas Y. Crowell Co., 1961).

Lineberry, Robert L., and Ira Sharkansky. Urban Politics and Public Policy (New York: Harper & Row, Publishers, 1971).

Linowes, R. Robert, and Don T. Allensworth. The Politics of Land Use (New York: Praeger Publishers, 1973).

McClosky, Clifton. The Government and Politics of Texas, 3rd ed. (Boston: Little, Brown and Co., 1969).

Mannino, E.F., "Strengthening Citizen Input under the National Environmental Policy Act," Pennsylvania Bar Association Quarterly, Vol. 45, No. 4 (June 1974), pp. 411-22.

Martin, Roscoe C. The Cities and the Federal System (New York: Atherton Press, 1965).

Merelman, Richard M. "On the Neo-Elitist Critique of Community Power," American Political Science Review, Vol. 62, No. 2 (June 1968), pp. 451-60.

Milbraith, L.W. Political Participation: How and Why Do People Get Involved in Politics (Chicago: Rand McNally and Co., 1965).

Moynihan, Daniel P. "The Relationship of Federal to Local Authorities," Daedalus, Vol. 96, No. 3 (Summer, 1967), pp. 801-08.

Mumphrey, Anthony J., Jr., John E. Seley, and Julian Wolpert. "A Decision Model for Locating Controversial Facilities," Journal of the American Institute of Planners, Vol. 37, No. 6 (November 1971), pp. 397-402.

Oakland Task Force, San Francisco Federal Executive Board. Federal Decision-Making and Impact in Urban Areas: A Study of Oakland (New York: Praeger Publishers, 1970).

Perloff, Harvey S. "Modernizing Urban Development," Daedalus, Vol. 96, No. 3 (Summer 1967), pp. 789-800.

Polsby, Nelson W. Community Power and Political Theory (New Haven: Yale University Press, 1963).

Rourke, Francis E. Bureaucracy, Politics, and Public Policy (Boston: Little, Brown and Co., 1969).

Schattschneider, E. E. The Semi-Sovereign People (New York: Holt, Rinehart and Winston, 1960).

Stedman, Murray S., Jr. Urban Politics (Cambridge, Mass.: Winthrop Publishers, 1972).

Stevens, Joseph L. The Impact of Federal Legislation and Programs on Private Land in Urban and Metropolitan Development (New York: Praeger Publishers, 1973).

Texas Legislature. Texas Water Quality Act of 1967, Tex. Rev. Civ. Stat. Ann. arts. 21.001-21.612 (1972); Acts 1967, 60th Legis., p. 745, ch. 313, amend. 1969, 1971, Austin, Tex.

Truman, David B. The Governmental Process, (New York: Alfred A. Knopf, 1955).

U.S. Congress. National Environmental Policy Act of 1969, P. L. 91-190, 42 U.S.C. 4321 et seq., Washington, D. C.

U.S. Department of Housing and Urban Development. Department Policies, Responsibilities and Procedures for Protection and Enhancement of Environmental Quality, Circular 1390.1 (July 1971); revised (April 1972); revised (December 1972); Washington, D. C.

U.S. Office of Management and Budget, Circular A-95 (July 24, 1969); revised (February 9, 1971); revised (November 13, 1973); Washington, D. C.

U.S. Senate, Committee on Rules and Administration, Study of Intergovernmental Relationships, Senate Report No. 967 (Washington, D. C.: U.S. Senate, The Committee, 89th Congr. 2nd Sess., February 1966).

Williams, Oliver P., and Charles R. Adrian. Four Cities: A Study in Comparative Policy-Making (Philadelphia: University of Pennsylvania Press, 1963).

Wilson, James Q., ed. City Politics and Public Policy (New York: John Wiley & Sons, 1968).

Wolfinger, Raymond E. "Nondecisions and the Study of Local Politics," American Political Science Review, Vol. 65, No. 4 (December 1971), pp. 1063-80.

Wolpert, Julian (Principal Investigator). Research on Conflict in Locational Decisions, Discussion Paper Series (Philadelphia: Regional Science Department, University of Pennsylvania, 1970).

The Texas Observer (miscellaneous articles), Austin, Texas.

New Communities

Advisory Commission on Intergovernmental Relations, Urban and Rural America: Policies for Future Growth (Washington, D.C.: The Commission, April 1968).

Allen, Muriel I., ed. The AIP Task Force on New Communities, New Communities: Challenge for Today, Background Paper—No. 2 (Washington, D.C.: American Institute of Planners, 1968).

Alonso, William. "What Are New Towns For?" Urban Studies, Vol. 7, No. 1 (February 1970), pp. 37-55.

"Are New Towns Old Hat? U.S. Said to Lean Toward a Phase-Out," House and Home, Vol. 46, No. 2 (August 1974), p. 9.

Bodnar, Donald J., and Mark Wassenich. Implementation: A Critical Limit on the Planner's Role in Planned Community Development, Research Memorandum (Chapel Hill: Center for Urban and Regional Studies, University of North Carolina, May 1970).

Boykin, Hamilton H., and James C. Brincefield, Jr. "The Federal New Communities Program: Comments on the Legislation, Processing, and Documentation," The Urban Lawyer, Vol. 4, No. 2 (Spring 1972), pp. 189-205.

Burke, Barlow Jr., and Thomas Dienes. "Creating a Community: Process of Land Development for Urban Growth," Houston Law Review, Vol. 9, No. 2 (November 1971), pp. 189-270.

Cartsonis, Emanuel M. "New Towns: A Challenge to Partnership of Private and Public Enterprise," Planning, 1967 (Chicago: American Society of Planning Officials, 1967), pp. 174-77.

Christensen, Boake. "Land Use Control for the New Community," Harvard Journal on Legislation, Vol. 6, No. 4 (May 1969), pp. 496-547.

Clapp, James A. "The First (and Last?) Meeting of the Regional New Towns Committee," City, Vol. 5, No. 6 (Winter 1971), pp. 42-47.

____. New Towns and Urban Policy (New York: Dunellen Publishing Co., 1971).

____. "Potentially 'Counter-Intuitive' Elements in Federal New Communities Legislation," San Diego Law Review, Vol. 9, No. 1 (December 1971), p. 1.

Comment, "Democracy in the New Towns: The Limits of Private Government," University of Chicago Law Review, Vol. 36, No. 2 (Winter 1969), pp. 379-412.

Comptroller General of the U.S., Getting the New Communities Programs Started (Washington, D.C.: Government Accounting Office, November 1974).

Connell, Kathleen M. Regional New Towns and Intergovernmental Relations: Four Case Studies (Detroit: Metropolitan Fund, Inc., 1972).

DeLucia, Francis C. "New Communities and Small Town America," The Urban Lawyer: Vol. 4, No. 4 (Fall 1972), pp. 734-45.

Derthick, Martha. "Defeat at Fort Lincoln," The Public Interest, No. 20 (Summer 1970), pp. 3-39.

____. New Towns In-Town (Washington, D.C.: The Urban Institute, 1972).

Eichler, Edward P., and Marshall Kaplan. The Community Builders (Berkeley: University of California Press, 1967).

Gasaway, Laura Nell. "New Community Development Districts: A Proposal to Aid New Town Developers," Houston Law Review, Vol. 9, No. 5 (May 1972), pp. 1032-77.

Gibson, John H., and Douglas G. Simms. "New Community Development," Washburn Law Review, Vol. 11, No. 2 (Winter 1972), pp. 227-50.

Gliege, John G. New Towns: Policy Problems in Regulating Development, Papers in Public Administration No. 17 (Tempe, Ariz.: Institute for Public Administration, Arizona State University, 1970).

Godschalk, David R. "Reforming New Community Planning," Journal of the American Institute of Planners, Vol. 39, No. 5 (September 1973), pp. 306-15.

Golany, Gideon and Daniel Walden, eds., The Contemporary New Communities Movement in the United States (Urbana: University of Illinois Press, 1974).

Jackson, Samuel C. "Address to Secretary's Workshop on New Communities," Holiday Inn, Silver Spring, Md., October 24, 1972.

____. "New Communities," HUD Challenge, Vol. 3, No. 8 (August 1972), pp. 4-7.

Keegan, John E., and William Rutzick. "Private Developers and the New Communities Act of 1968," Georgetown Law Journal, Vol. 57, No. 6 (June 1969), pp. 1019-58.

Logue, Edward J. "Piecing the Political Pie," in "New Communities: Business on the Urban Frontier," (Special Issue), Saturday Review, Vol. 54, No. 20 (May 15, 1971), pp. 27-29ff.

McAllister, Bill. "A 'Soul City' in the Carolina Piedmont," Norfolk Virginian-Pilot, July 16, 1972.

Metropolitan Washington Council of Governments, New Communities in Metropolitan Areas: The Governmental Role (Washington, D.C.: The Council, 1970).

Meyer, Lawrence. "County Coolness Imperils New Town," Washington Post, January 10, 1972.

Morris, Robert L. "New Towns and Old Cities," Nation's Cities.
Part I: "The Impact of New Towns," April 1969, pp. 8-11;
Part II: "What Can the Cities Learn from the New Town Experience?" May 1969, pp. 19-22; Part III: "Prospects for Coexistence," June 1969, pp. 39-42.

Mullarkey, Mary J. "The Evolution of a New Community: Problems of Government," Harvard Journal on Legislation, Vol. 6, No. 4 (May 1969), pp. 462-95.

New Jersey Department of Community Affairs. New Communities Policy and Development in the U.S.: A Fifty State Survey (Trenton, N.J.: New Communities Section, Division of State and Regional Planning, Department of Community Affairs, State of New Jersey, 1973).

Nunn, Douglas, ed. NewCom: The Enabling Elements, Vol. IV of The New Communities Family Mobility System and the NewCom Demonstration (Louisville: The Urban Studies Center, University of Louisville, 1971).

O'Mara, Paul. "Citizen Participation Sought in New Towns," Planning, Vol. 38, No. 11 (December 1972), pp. 300-02.

Perloff, Harvey S., and Neil C. Sandberg, eds., New Towns: Why—And for Whom? (New York: Praeger Publishers, 1973).

Schulman, S.J., "The Public's Response: Planning For and Against Development," Land Use Controls, I, No. 2 (1967) pp. 20-26.

Scott, Stanley, "The Large New Communities: Ultimate Self-Government and Other Problems," Public Affairs Report, Institute of Governmental Studies, University of California, Berkeley, Vol. 6, No. 5 (October 1965).

____. "The Large New Communities and Urban Growth: A Broad Perspective and its Implications," Public Affairs Report, Institute of Governmental Studies, University of California, Berkeley, Vol. 6, No. 6 (December 1965).

____. "Local Government and the New Communities," Public Affairs Report, Institute of Governmental Studies, University of California, Berkeley, Vol. 6, No. 3 (June 1965).

_____. Local Government for Large New Communities, Institute of Governmental Studies, University of California, Berkeley, 1965 (unpublished).

_____. New Towns Development and the Role of Government, Institute of Governmental Studies, University of California, Berkeley, 1964 (unpublished).

"Soul City," Newsweek, August 14, 1972, pp. 23-24.

Twentieth Century Fund Task Force on Governance of New Towns, New Towns: Laboratories for Democracy, Background paper by Royce Hanson (New York: Twentieth Century Fund, 1971).

U.S. Congress. Housing and Urban Development Act of 1970, P.L. 91-609, Title VII (Urban Growth and New Community Development Act), 42 U.S.C. 4501 et seq., Washington, D.C.

U.S. Department of Housing and Urban Development. Draft Regulations: Assistance for New Communities (Urban Growth and New Community Development Act of 1970), 24 CFR 720 (August 7, 1972); revised from Draft Regulations, 24 CFR 32 (July 31, 1971); Washington, D.C.

Weiss, Shirley F., Edward J. Kaiser, and Raymond J. Burby, III, eds. New Community Development: Planning Process, Implementation, and Emerging Social Concerns, Vol. 1 and 2 (Chapel Hill: New Towns Research Seminar, Center for Urban and Regional Studies, University of North Carolina, 1971).

League of New Community Developers, News of the Week (various issues), League of New Community Developers, Washington, D.C. (1972-    ).

Urban Life in New and Renewing Communities (various issues), American City Corporation, Columbia, Md. (1970-    ).

WAYT T. WATTERSON was formerly Principal Planner in charge of the Long-Range Planning Section in the City of San Antonio Planning and Community Development Department. He was responsible for studies concerning population, neighborhood planning, annexation, and future growth patterns. Previously he was associated with the Washington-based consulting firm of Leo Kramer, Inc., and the Cleveland real estate appraisal firm of Chester S. Giltz and Associates.

Mr. Watterson has a master's degree in regional planning from the University of North Carolina at Chapel Hill and a B.A. degree from Williams College. He is presently pursuing a doctorate in city and regional planning at the University of Pennsylvania.

ROBERTA S. WATTERSON is a Senior Housing Analyst with the City of Philadelphia. Previously she was an independent planning consultant specializing in economic research. She was formerly affiliated with Gladstone Associates of Washington, D.C., where she carried out market analyses and project planning for a number of large-scale real estate developments, including San Antonio Ranch New Town.

Ms. Watterson holds a master's degree in community and regional planning from the University of Texas at Austin and a B.A. degree from the University of Massachusetts.

ARE NEW TOWNS FOR LOWER INCOME
AMERICANS TOO?

> edited by
> John C. DeBoer
> Alexander Greendale

THE POLITICAL REALITIES OF URBAN PLANNING
> Don T. Allensworth

ECONOMICS AND NEW TOWNS: A Comparative
Study of the United States, the United Kingdom,
and Australia

> Albert J. Robinson

LAND USE AND THE GOVERNMENT PROCESS:
The San Francisco Bay Area Experience

> edited by
> Edward Ellis Smith
> Durward S. Riggs